THIS DAY AND AGE

An Anthology of Modern Poetry in English

selected by

STANLEY HEWETT, B.A.

LONDON
EDWARD ARNOLD (PUBLISHERS) LTD.

The picture on the cover is reproduced
by permission of the *Radio Times Hulton
Picture Library*

PRINTED IN GREAT BRITAIN IN THE CITY OF OXFORD
AT THE ALDEN PRESS

INTRODUCTION

In spite of the obvious relevance of twentieth-century literature to twentieth-century readers, distressingly few children in schools today have an opportunity of reading the poetry which comes from their own environment. They are mostly concerned with poetry which arose in worlds totally different from the one they know. These voices from the past, speaking of an unfamiliar world in an unfamiliar language, frequently arouse a luke-warm response in children, who, together with their teachers, might well be more profitably concerned with the stimulus and challenge of modern literature.

This neglect of contemporary verse in schools is due partly to the lack of suitable editions and partly to a suspicion on the part of teachers that such verse is unsuitable for children, either because of its impenetrable obscurity, or because of its frank clarity. It is hoped that this collection of poems written since 1919 will go some way towards removing both difficulties.

A great deal of twentieth-century poetry is undoubtedly beyond the emotional and intellectual grasp of children — so is much of the poetry of any century. Nor is it denied that the poems which follow demand as much from the reader as he or she is capable of giving — that is true of any poem ever written. It is denied, however, that modern poetry, as distinct from earlier poetry, makes demands upon its readers that modern children are unable to meet. Children accustomed to the sophisticated techniques now current in radio, television, film and advertising are capable of taking in their stride any problems of communication with which modern poetry presents them, provided that reasonable care is exercised in the selection of material and that it is approached without the prejudice that comes from preconceived ideas.

However posterity will judge poetry written in this period at least its writers have the merit of being intensely concerned with life as it is being lived. The poems in this anthology not only have merit as verse, but also represent ideas, feelings, arguments and attitudes which can stimulate thought not exclusively literary. There is a content to which the reader can respond, not just an object for academic examination, though this is not precluded if it is desired. The chorus from T. S. Eliot's *The Rock*, for example, should lead to a consideration, not only of the poet's language and versification, but also of the 'decent godless people' and the 'litter of Sunday newspapers'.

Though the poems in this collection were chosen on their merits and were not intended to represent an outline literary or social history of the period, they in fact do both. These poets have written of the things that interested and moved them at various times and in so doing they have represented their age as no historian could. Under the mass of individual variations of content, form and style the major preoccupations of each decade find expression and, in addition, the form of that expression can be seen in a continuous process of transition and development. To assist those readers who prefer a systematic study of authors or periods to random browsing the poems have been arranged according to country of origin within which they are grouped under authors who appear in roughly chronological order inside their national divisions. To continue the education of the English out of their intolerant attitude towards the American language (see *England Expects* by Ogden Nash, page 119) all American poems retain the American spellings and grammatical forms used by their authors.

The wide range of American and Commonwealth representation, even within the limits of this selection, should encourage children to think in terms of a literature in English rather than English literature. This in itself may help them to understand that the superficial differences between people are less striking than their fundamental similarities. Poetry, which, by its very nature, gives vivid and permanent expression to the thoughts and feelings of mankind, is the ideal medium for such learning.

A note on Notes

These have been used sparingly throughout. They are intended to give the optimum help and the minimum distraction to a child reading alone, rather than with the class, since such individual work is now a feature of many secondary schools. They are not intended to usurp the function of the teacher when the class is working as a unit under his guidance.

*   *   *

'Why is it that the latest poet has generally the greatest influence over the minds of the young? Surely not for the mere charm of novelty? The reason is that he, living amid the same hopes, the same temptations, the same sphere of observation as they, gives utterance and outward form to the very questions which, vague and wordless, have been exercising their hearts ... True, all great poets are by their office democrats; seers of man only as man; singers of the joys, the sorrows, the aspirations common to all humanity.'

Alton Locke Charles Kingsley

TABLE OF CONTENTS

Arranged alphabetically by Authors   PAGE

A*   ix

CONTENTS

CONTENTS

xi

CONTENTS

CONTENTS

THIS DAY AND AGE

It is unusual to begin with an epitaph, yet this poem by a young West Indian poet summarizes so well the anxieties, hopes and fears of the world since 1918, that it is, perhaps, appropriate. Like much of the poetry that follows, it holds a note of sadness, but it is the sadness of frustrated hope rather than hopelessness. If we reach out 'for the very stars themselves' some disappointment is almost inevitable. That is no reason for not 'reaching'.

Epitaph

I think they will remember this as the age of lamentations,
The age of broken minds and broken souls,
The age of hurt creatures sobbing out their sorrow to the
    rhythm of the blues —
The music of lost Africa's desolation become the music of the
    town.

The age of failure of splendid things,
The age of the deformity of splendid things,
The age of old young men and bitter children,
The age of treachery and of a great new faith.
The age of madness and machines,
Of broken bodies and fear twisted hearts,

The age of frenzied fumbling and possessive lusts —
And yet, deep down, an age unsatisfied by dirt and guns,
An age which though choked by the selfishness of the few who
    owned their bodies and their souls,

Still struggled blindly to the end,
And in their time reached out magnificently
Even for the very stars themselves.

H. D. Carberry

To the Public

A poet is often imagined to be a shy, sensitive creature who shrinks from life as it is lived by the majority of people. How does this picture compare with Louis Macneice's self-portrait?

Why hold that poets are so sensitive?
A thickskinned grasping lot who filch and eavesdrop,
Who enjoy ourselves at other men's expense,
Who, legislators or not, ourselves are lawless,
We do not need your indulgence, much less your pity;
With fewer qualms, we have rather more common sense
Than your Common Man, also of course more freedom,
With our burglars' and gunmen's fingers, our green fingers.
So, crude though we are, we get to times and places
And, saving your presence or absence, will continue
Throwing our dreams and guts in people's faces.

Louis Macneice

Chorus from The Rock

This poem is from the pageant play of that name.

The Word of the LORD came unto me, saying:
O miserable cities of designing men,
O wretched generation of enlightened men,
Betrayed in the mazes of your ingenuities,
Sold by the proceeds of your proper inventions:
I have given you hands which you turn from worship,
I have given you speech, for endless palaver,

I have given you my Law, and you set up commissions,
I have given you lips, to express friendly sentiments,
I have given you hearts, for reciprocal distrust.
I have given you power of choice, and you only alternate
Between futile speculation and unconsidered action.
Many are engaged in writing books and printing them,
Many desire to see their names in print,
Many read nothing but the race reports.
Much is your reading, but not the Word of GOD,
Much is your building, but not the House of GOD.
Will you build me a house of plaster, with corrugated roofing,
To be filled with a litter of Sunday newspapers?

FIRST MALE VOICE:
A Cry from the East:
What shall be done to the shore of smoky ships?
Will you leave my people forgetful and forgotten
To idleness, labour, and delirious stupor?
There shall be left the broken chimney,
The peeled hull, a pile of rusty iron,
In a street of scattered brick where the goat climbs,
Where my Word is unspoken.

SECOND MALE VOICE:
A Cry from the North, from the West and from the South
Whence thousands travel daily to the timekept City;
Where My Word is unspoken,
In the land of lobelias and tennis flannels
The rabbit shall burrow and the thorn revisit,
The nettle shall flourish on the gravel court,
And the wind shall say: 'Here were decent godless people:
Their only monument the asphalt road
And a thousand lost golf balls.'

CHORUS:

We build in vain unless the LORD build with us.
Can you keep the City that the LORD keeps not with you?
A thousand policemen directing the traffic
Cannot tell you why you come or where you go.
A colony of cavies or a horde of active marmots
Build better than they that build without the LORD.
Shall we lift up our feet among perpetual ruins?
I have loved the beauty of Thy House, the peace of Thy sanc-
tuary,
I have swept the floors and garnished the altars.
Where there is no temple there shall be no homes,
Though you have shelters and institutions,
Precarious lodgings while the rent is paid,
Subsiding basements where the rat breeds
Or sanitary dwellings with numbered doors
Or a house a little better than your neighbour's;
When the Stranger says: 'What is the meaning of this city?
Do you huddle close together because you love each other?'
What will you answer? 'We all dwell together
To make money from each other'? or 'This is a community'?
And the Stranger will depart and return to the desert.
O my soul, be prepared for the coming of the Stranger,
Be prepared for him who knows how to ask questions.

O weariness of men who turn from GOD
To the grandeur of your mind and the glory of your action,
To arts and inventions and daring enterprises,
To schemes of human greatness thoroughly discredited,
Binding the earth and the water to your service,
Exploiting the seas and developing the mountains,
Dividing the stars into common and preferred,

4

Engaged in devising the perfect refrigerator,
Engaged in working out a rational morality,
Engaged in printing as many books as possible,
Plotting of happiness and flinging empty bottles,
Turning from your vacancy to fevered enthusiasm
For nation or race or what you call humanity;
Though you forget the way to the Temple,
There is one who remembers the way to your door:
Life you may evade, but Death you shall not.
You shall not deny the Stranger.

T. S. Eliot

The Dry Salvages — IV

This poem is a short section from The Dry Salvages *which in turn forms one of the* Four Quartets.

The Dry Salvages (rhymes with 'rages') is a small group of rocks off the north-east coast of Cape Ann, Massachusetts, U.S.A. The origin of the name is uncertain: it may be an English 'version' of les trois sauvages.

Lady, whose shrine stands on the promontory,
Pray for all those who are in ships, those
Whose business has to do with fish, and
Those concerned with every lawful traffic
And those who conduct them.

Repeat a prayer also on behalf of
Women who have seen their sons or husbands
Setting forth, and not returning:
Figlia del tuo figlio,[1]
Queen of Heaven.

[1] 'Daughter of thy Son' i.e. the Virgin Mary.

5

Also pray for those who were in ships, and
Ended their voyage on the sand, in the sea's lips
Or in the dark throat which will not reject them
Or wherever cannot reach them the sound of the sea bell's
Perpetual angelus.

T. S. Eliot

Dialogue from The Ascent of F.6

This poem is taken from a play in verse and prose which Auden wrote in collaboration with his friend, Christopher Isherwood. F.6 was a mountain which a British expedition was to attempt to scale. This extract introduces Mr. and Mrs. A. who, from their sheltered suburban existence, follow the fortunes of the expedition through newspaper and radio reports.

MRS. A.   Evening. A slick and unctuous Time
Has sold us yet another shop-soiled day,
Patently rusty, not even in a gaudy box.
I have dusted the six small rooms:
The parlour, once the magnificent image of my free-
      dom,
And the bedroom, which once held for me
The mysterious languors of Egypt and the terrifying
      Indias.
The delivery-vans have paid their brief impersonal
      visits.
I have eaten a scrappy lunch from a plate on my knee.
I have spoken with acquaintances in the Stores;
Under our treble gossip heard the menacing throb of
      our hearts
As I hear them now, as all of us hear them,

Standing at our stoves in these villas, expecting our
    husbands:
The drums of an enormous and routed army,
Throbbing raggedly, fitfully, scatteredly, madly.
We are lost. We are lost.

(Enter Mr. A. *from work.)*

MR. A.   Has anything happened?

MRS. A.   What should happen?
The cat has died at Ivy Dene,
The Crowthers' pimply son has passed Matric,
St. Neots has put up light blue curtains,
Frankie is walking out with Winnie
And Georgie loves himself. What should happen?
Nothing that matters will ever happen.

MR. A.   No, nothing that matters will ever happen;
Nothing you'd want to put in a book;
Nothing to tell to impress your friends —
The old old story that never ends:
The eight o'clock train, the customary place,
Holding the paper in front of your face,
The public stairs, the glass swing-door,
The peg for your hat, the linoleum floor,
The office stool and the office jokes
And the fear in your ribs that slyly pokes:
Are they satisfied with you?
Nothing interesting to do,
Nothing interesting to say,
Nothing remarkable in any way;
Then the journey home again
In the hot suburban train
To the tawdry new estate,
Crumpled, grubby, dazed and late:

7

Home to supper and to bed.
Shall we be like this when we are dead?

W. H. Auden

Chorus from The Dog beneath the Skin

This extract is the opening of the play and sets the bitter, angry mood that prevails throughout its action.

CHORUS
The Summer holds: upon its glittering lake
Lie Europe and the islands; many rivers
Wrinkling its surface like a ploughman's palm.
Under the bellies of the grazing horses
On the far side of posts and bridges
The vigorous shadows dwindle; nothing wavers.
Calm at this moment the Dutch sea so shallow
That sunk St. Paul's would ever show its golden cross
And still the deep water that divides us still from Norway.
We would show you at first an English village: You shall choose
      its location
Wherever your heart directs you most longingly to look; you
      are loving towards it:
Whether north to Scots Gap and Bellingham where the black
      rams defy the panting engine:
Or west to the Welsh Marches; to the lilting speech and the
      magicians' faces:
Wherever you were a child or had your first affair
There it stands amidst your darling scenery:
A parish bounded by the wreckers' cliff; or meadows where
      browse the Shorthorn and the maplike Friesian

8

As at Trent Junction where the Soar comes gliding; out of green
　　Leicestershire to swell the ampler current.

Hiker with sunburn blisters on your office pallor,
Cross-country champion with corks in your hands,
When you have eaten your sandwich, your salt and your apple,
When you have begged your glass of milk from the ill-kept
　　farm,
What is it you see?

I see barns falling, fences broken,
Pasture not ploughland, weeds not wheat.
The great houses remain but only half are inhabited,
Dusty the gunrooms and the stable clocks stationary.
Some have been turned into prep-schools where the diet is
　　in the hands of an experienced matron,
Others into club-houses for the golf-bore and the top-hole.
Those who sang in the inns at evening have departed; they saw
　　their hope in another country,
Their children have entered the service of the suburban areas;
　　they have become typists, mannequins and factory opera-
　　tives; they desired a different rhythm of life.
But their places are taken by another population, with views
　　about nature,
Brought in charabanc and saloon along arterial roads;
Tourists to whom the Tudor cafés
Offer Bovril and buns upon Breton ware
With leather work as a sideline: Filling stations
Supplying petrol from rustic pumps.
Those who fancy themselves as foxes or desire a special setting
　　for spooning
Erect their villas at the right places,
Airtight, lighted, *e*laborately warmed;

9

And nervous people who will never marry
Live upon dividends in the old-world cottages
With an animal for friend or a volume of memoirs.

Man is changed by his living; but not fast enough.
His concern today is for that which yesterday did not occur.
In the hour of the Blue Bird[1] and the Bristol Bomber,[2] his
    thoughts are appropriate to the years of the Penny Farthing:
He tosses at night who at noonday found no truth.

restlessness – has not found peace.

W. H. Auden

The Unknown Citizen

(To JS/07/M378 This Marble Monument is Erected by the State)

He was found by the Bureau of Statistics to be
One against whom there was no official complaint,
And all the reports on his conduct agree
That, in the modern sense of an old-fashioned word, he was a
    saint,
For in everything he did he served the Greater Community.
Except for the War till the day he retired   *monotony*
He worked in a factory and never got fired,
But satisfied his employers, Fudge Motors Inc. *exploited*   *mocking?*
Yet he wasn't a scab or odd in his views, *did belong to union*
For his Union reports that he paid his dues,
(Our report on his Union shows it was sound)
And our Social Psychology workers found
That he was popular with his mates and liked a drink.

---

[1] The name of the car in which Sir Malcolm Campbell set several world land
speed records.
[2] The Bristol 'Blenheim', then the last word in medium bombers.

The Press are convinced that he bought a paper every day
And that his reactions to advertisements were normal in every
way.
Policies taken out in his name prove that he was fully insured,
And his Health-card shows he was once in hospital but left it
cured.
Both Producers Research and High-Grade Living declare
He was fully sensible to the advantages of the Instalment Plan
And had everything necessary to the Modern Man,
A phonograph, a radio, a car and a frigidaire.
Our researchers into Public Opinion are content
That he held the proper opinions for the time of year;
When there was peace, he was for peace; when there was war,
he went.
He was married and added five children to the population,
Which our Eugenist says was the right number for a parent of
his generation,
And our teachers report that he never interfered with their
education.
Was he free? Was he happy? The question is absurd:
Had anything been wrong, we should certainly have heard.

W. H. Auden

The Express

After the first powerful, plain manifesto
The black statement of pistons, without more fuss
But gliding like a queen, she leaves the station.
Without bowing and with restrained unconcern
She passes the houses which humbly crowd outside,
The gasworks, and at last the heavy page
Of death, printed by gravestones in the cemetery.

Beyond the town, there lies the open country
Where, gathering speed, she acquires mystery,
The luminous self-possession of ships on ocean.
It is now she begins to sing — at first quite low
Then loud, and at last with a jazzy madness —
The song of her whistle screaming at curves,
Of deafening tunnels, brakes, innumerable bolts.
And always light, aerial, underneath,
Retreats the elate metre of her wheels.
Steaming through metal landscape on her lines,
She plunges new eras of white happiness,
Where speed throws up strange shapes, broad curves
And parallels clean like trajectories from guns.
At last, further than Edinburgh or Rome,
Beyond the crest of the world, she reaches night
Where only a low stream-line brightness
Of phosphorus on the tossing hills is light.
Ah, like a comet through flame, she moves entranced,
Wrapt in her music no bird song, no, nor bough
Breaking with honey buds, shall ever equal.

Stephen Spender

The Pylons

The secret of these hills was stone, and cottages
Of that stone made,
And crumbling roads
That turned on sudden hidden villages.

Now over these small hills, they have built the concrete
That trails black wire;
Pylons, those pillars
Bare like nude giant girls that have no secret.

The valley with its gilt and evening look
And the green chestnut
Of customary root,
Are mocked dry like the parched bed of a brook.

But far above and far as sight endures
Like whips of anger
With lightning's danger
There runs the quick perspective of the future.

This dwarfs our emerald country by its trek
So tall with prophecy:
Dreaming of cities
Where often clouds shall lean their swan-white neck.

Stephen Spender

★   ★   ★

The next two poems arose from Stephen Spender's visit to Spain during the bitter civil war which raged there in the 1930s. It was a terrifying blend of amateur and professional warfare in which almost every Spanish citizen, regardless of age or sex, was cruelly implicated.

Port Bou

As a child holds a pet
Arms clutching but with hands that do not join
And the coiled animal looks through the gap
To outer freedom animal air,
So the earth-and-rock arms of this small harbour
Embrace but do not encircle the sea
Which, through a gap, vibrates into the ocean,
Where dolphins swim and liners throb.

In the bright winter sunlight I sit on the parapet
Of a bridge; my circling arms rest on a newspaper
And my mind is empty as the glittering stone
While I search for an image
(The one written above) and the words (written above)
To set down the childish headlands of Port Bou.
A lorry halts beside me with creaking brakes
And I look up at warm downwards-looking faces
Of militia men staring at my (French) newspaper.
'How do they write of our struggle over the frontier?'
I hold out the paper, but they cannot read it,
They want speech and to offer cigarettes.
In their waving flag-like faces the war finds peace. The famished
    mouths
Of rusted carbines lean against their knees,
Like leaning, rust-coloured, fragile reeds.
Wrapped in cloth — old granny in a shawl —
The stuttering machine-gun rests.
They shout — salute back as the truck jerks forward
Over the vigorous hill, beyond the headland.
An old man passes, his mouth dribbling,
From three rusted teeth, he shoots out: 'pom-pom-pom'.
The children run after; and, more slowly, the women;
Clutching their skirts, trail over the horizon.
Now Port Bou is empty, for the firing practice.
I am left alone on the parapet at the exact centre
Above the river trickling through the gulley, like that old man's
    saliva.
The exact centre, solitary as the bull's eye in a target.
Nothing moves against the background of stage-scenery houses
Save the skirring mongrels. The firing now begins
Across the harbour mouth, from headland to headland,

White flecks of foam whipped by lead from the sea
An echo spreads its cat-o'-nine tails
Thrashing the flanks of neighbour hills.
My circling arms rest on the newspaper,
My mind is paper on which dust and words sift,
I assure myself the shooting is only for practice
But I am the coward of cowards. The machine-gun stitches
My intestines with a needle, back and forth;
The solitary, spasmodic, white puffs from the carbines
Draw fear in white threads back and forth through my body.

Stephen Spender

Ultima Ratio Regum[1]

The guns spell money's ultimate reason
In letters of lead on the Spring hillside.
But the boy lying dead under the olive trees
Was too young and too silly
To have been notable to their important eye.
He was a better target for a kiss.

When he lived, tall factory hooters never summoned him
Nor did restaurant plate-glass doors revolve to wave him in
His name never appeared in the papers.
The world maintained its traditional wall
Round the dead with their gold sunk deep as a well,
Whilst his life, intangible as a Stock Exchange rumour, drifted
    outside.

[1] The last argument of kings.

15

O too lightly he threw down his cap
One day when the breeze threw petals from the trees.
The unflowering wall sprouted with guns,
Machine-gun anger quickly scythed the grasses;
Flags and leaves fell from hands and branches;
The tweed cap rotted in the nettles.

Consider his life which was valueless
In terms of employment, hotel ledgers, news files.
Consider. One bullet in ten thousand kills a man.
Ask. Was so much expenditure justified
On the death of one so young, and so silly
Lying under the olive trees, O world, O death?

Stephen Spender

*   *   *

Though the next three poems — from The Magnetic Mountain —
*were written almost thirty years ago, they exhibit all the impatience
with the older generation that some young people feel to-day. The
'Angry Young Man' is not a discovery of the Atomic Age.*

The Magnetic Mountain

Part I

2

Parents

But Two there are, shadow us everywhere
And will not let us be till we are dead,
Hardening the bones, keeping the spirit spare,
Original in water, earth and air,
Our bitter cordial, our daily bread.

16

Turning over old follies in ante-room,
For first-born waiting or for late reprieve,
Watching the safety-valve, the slackening loom,
Abed, abroad, at every turn and tomb
A shadow starts, a hand is on your sleeve.

O you, my comrade, now or to-morrow flayed
Alive, crazed by the nibbling nerve; my friend
Whom hate has cornered or whom love betrayed,
By hunger sapped, trapped by a stealthy tide,
Brave for so long but whimpering in the end:

Such are the temporal princes, fear and pain,
Whose borders march with the ice-fields of death,
And from that servitude escape there's none
Till in the grave we set up house alone
And buy our liberty with our last breath.

C. Day Lewis

The Magnetic Mountain

Part II

9

In this passage Cecil Day Lewis is ironically defending the English middle class and being sarcastic about the Public School system with its 'right types' and 'done things'. He feels that the system is dying but expects its products, as befits their training, to do the 'decent thing' at the funeral.

Second Defendant speaks
      Let us now praise famous men,
      Not your earth-shakers, not the dynamiters,

17

But who in the Home Counties or the Khyber,
Trimming their nails to meet an ill wind,
Facing the Adversary with a clean collar,
Justified the system.
Admire the venerable pile that bred them,
Bones are its foundations,
The pinnacles are stone abstractions,
Whose halls are whispering-galleries designed
To echo voices of the past, dead tongues.
White hopes of England here
Are taught to rule by learning to obey,
Bend over before vested interests,
Kiss the rod, salute the quarter-deck;
Here is no savage discipline
Of peregrine swooping, of fire destroying,
But a civil code; no capital offender
But the cool cad, the man who goes too far.
Ours the curriculum
Neither of building birds nor wasteful waters,
Bound in book not violent in vein:
Here we inoculate with dead ideas
Against blood-epidemics, against
The infection of faith and the excess of life.
Our methods are up to date; we teach
Through head and not by heart,
Language with gramophones and sex with charts,
Prophecy by deduction, prayer by numbers.
For honours see prospectus: those who leave us
Will get a post and pity the poor;
Their eyes glaze at strangeness;
They are never embarrassed, have a word for everything,
Living on credit, dying when the heart stops;

Will wear black armlets and stand a moment in silence
For the passing of an era, at their own funeral.

C. Day Lewis

The Magnetic Mountain

Part III

25

Consider these, for we have condemned them;
Leaders to no sure land, guides their bearings lost
Or in league with robbers have reversed the signposts,
Disrespectful to ancestors, irresponsible to heirs.
Born barren, a freak growth, root in rubble,
Fruitlessly blossoming, whose foliage suffocates,
Their sap is sluggish, they reject the sun.

The man with his tongue in his cheek, the woman
With her heart in the wrong place, unhandsome, unwholesome;
Have exposed the new-born to worse than weather,
Exiled the honest and sacked the seer.
These drowned the farms to form a pleasure-lake,
In time of drought they drain the reservoir
Through private pipes for baths and sprinklers.

Getters not begetters; gainers not beginners;
Whiners, no winners; no triers, betrayers;
Who steer by no star, whose moon means nothing.
Daily denying, unable to dig:
At bay in villas from blood relations,
Counters of spoons and content with cushions
They pray for peace, they hand down disaster.

They that take the bribe shall perish by the bribe,
Dying of dry rot, ending in asylums,
A curse to children, a charge on the state.
But still their fears and frenzies infect us;
Drug nor isolation will cure this cancer:
It is now or never, the hour of the knife,
The break with the past, the major operation.

C. Day Lewis

The Misfit

At the training depot that first morning
When the west-country draft came forth on parade —
Mechanics, labourers, men of trade
Herded with shouts like boneheaded cattle —
One stood out from the maul
Who least of them all
Looked metal for killing or meat for the butchery blade.

He wore a long black cutaway coat
Which should have been walking by blackthorn-fleeced
Hedges to church; and good as a feast
Was the spare, wild face much weather had flavoured.
A shepherd or ploughman
I thought, or a cowman —
One with a velvet hand for all manner of beast.

I cannot forget how he stood, bemused,
With the meek eye of a driven thing:
But a solitude old as a cromlech ring
Was around him; a freeborn air of the downland,

20

A peace of deep combes
No world-anger consumes
Marked him off from the herd to be branded for soldiering.

I saw him not after. Is he now buried
Far from pastures buttercup-strewed,
Or tending his beasts again with the same rude
Rightness of instinct which then had brought him
So quaintly dressed
In his Sunday best
For the first step along the Calvary road?

C. Day Lewis

Two Travellers

One of us in the compartment stares
Out of his window the whole day long
With attentive mien, as if he knows
There is hid in the journeying scene a song
To recall or compose
From snatches of vision, hints of vanishing airs.

He'll mark the couched hares
In grass whereover the lapwing reel and twist:
He notes how the shockheaded sunflowers climb
Like boys on the wire by the railway line;
And for him those morning rivers are love-in-a-mist,
And the chimneystacks prayers.

The other is plainly a man of affairs,
A seasoned commuter. His looks assert,
As he opens a briefcase intent on perusing

21

Facts and figures, he'd never divert
With profitless musing
The longest journey, or notice the dress it wears.

Little he cares
For the coloured drift of his passage: no, not a thing
Values in all that is hurrying past,
Though dimly he senses from first to last
How flaps and waves the smoke of his travelling
At the window-squares.

One is preoccupied, one just stares,
While the whale-ribbed terminus nears apace
Where passengers all must change, and under
Its arch triumphal quickly disperse.
So you may wonder,
Watching these two whom the train indifferently bears,

What each of them shares
With his fellow-traveller, and which is making the best of it,
And whether this or the other one
Will be justified when the journey's done,
And if either may carry on some reward or regret for it
Whither he fares.

C. Day Lewis

A Hard Frost

A frost came in the night and stole my world
And left this changeling for it — a precocious
Image of spring, too brilliant to be true:
White lilac on the windowpane, each grass-blade

Furred like a catkin, maydrift loading the hedge.
The elms behind the house are elms no longer
But blossomers in crystal, stems of the mist
That hangs yet in the valley below, amorphous
As the blind tissue whence creation formed.
　　The sun looks out, and the fields blaze with diamonds.
Mockery spring, to lend this bridal gear
For a few hours to a raw country maid,
Then leave her all disconsolate with old fairings
Of aconite and snowdrop! No, not here
Amid this flounce and filigree of death
Is the real transformation scene in progress,
But deep below where frost
Worrying the stiff clods unclenches their
Grip on the seed and lets our future breathe.

C. Day Lewis

Prayer before Birth

I am not yet born; O hear me.
Let not the bloodsucking bat or the rat or the stoat or the
　　club-footed ghoul come near me.

I am not yet born, console me
I fear that the human race may with tall walls wall me,
　　with strong drugs dope me, with wise lies lure me,
　　　　on black racks rack me, in blood-baths roll me.

I am not yet born; provide me
With water to dandle me, grass to grow for me, trees to talk
　　to me, sky to sing to me, birds and a white light
　　　　in the back of my mind to guide me.

I am not yet born; forgive me
For the sins that in me the world shall commit, my words
    when they speak me, my thoughts when they think me,
        my treason engendered by traitors beyond me,
           my life when they murder by means of my
             hands, my death when they live me.

I am not yet born; rehearse me
In the parts I must play and the cues I must take when
    old men lecture me, bureaucrats hector me, mountains
        frown at me, lovers laugh at me, the white
           waves call me to folly and the desert calls
             me to doom and the beggar refuses
                my gift and my children curse me.

I am not yet born; O hear me,
Let not the man who is beast or who thinks he is God come near
    me.

I am not yet born; O fill me
With strength against those who would freeze my
    humanity, would dragoon me into a lethal automaton,
        would make me a cog in a machine, a thing with
           one face, a thing, and against all those who
             would dissipate my entirety, would
                blow me like thistledown hither
                    and thither or hither and thither
                    like water held in the
                      hands would spill me.

Let them not make me a stone and let them not spill me.
Otherwise kill me.

Louis Macneice

Christmas Shopping

Spending beyond their income on gifts for Christmas —
Swing doors and crowded lifts and draperied jungles —
What shall we buy for our husbands and sons
    Different from last year?

Foxes hang by their noses behind plate glass —
Scream of macaws across festoons of paper —
Only the faces on the boxes of chocolates are free
    From boredom and crowsfeet.

Sometimes a chocolate box girl escapes in the flesh,
Lightly manœuvres the crowd, trilling with laughter;
After a couple of years her feet and her brain will
    Tire like the others.

The great windows marshal their troops for assault on the purse,
Something-and-eleven the yard, hoodwinking logic,
The eleventh hour draining the gurgling pennies
    Down the conduits

Down to the sewers of money — rats and marshgas —
Bubbling in maundering music under the pavement;
Here go the hours of routine, the weight on our eyelids —
    Pennies on corpses,

While over the street in the centrally heated public
Library dwindling figures with sloping shoulders
And hands in pockets, weighted in the boots like chessmen,
    Stare at the printed

Columns of ads, the quickset road to riches,
Starting at a little and temporary but once we're
Started who knows whether we shan't continue,
    Salaries rising,

powerful

Rising like a salmon against the bullnecked river,
Bound for the spawning-ground of care-free days —
Good for a fling before the golden wheels run
    Down to a standstill.   *money*   *society*

And Christ is born — the nursery glad with baubles,
Alive with light and washable paint and children's
Eyes expects as its due the accidental
    Loot of a system.

Smell of the South — oranges in silver paper,   *benediction or*
Dates and ginger, the benison of firelight,   *blessing*
The blue flames dancing round the brandied raisins,
    Smiles from above them,

Hands from above them as of gods but really
These their parents, always seen from below, them-
Selves are always anxious looking across the
    Fence to the future —

Out there lies the future gathering quickly
Its blank momentum; through the tubes of London
The dead winds blow the crowds like beasts in flight from
    Fire in the forest.

The little firtrees palpitate with candles
In hundreds of chattering households where the suburb

Straggles like nervous handwriting, the margin
    Blotted with smokestacks.

Further out on the coast the lighthouse moves its
Arms of light through the fog that wads our welfare,
Moves its arms like a giant at Swedish drill[1] whose
    Mind is a vacuum.

Louis Macneice

The British Museum Reading Room

*Not even the library staff knows exactly how many books are in
the British Museum Reading Room and Library. The approximate
total is between six and seven million and increasing daily. Its facilities
are unrivalled and scholars come from all parts of the world to study there.*

Under the hive-like dome the stooping haunted readers
Go up and down the alleys, tap the cells of knowledge —
    Honey and wax, the accumulation of years —
Some on commission, some for the love of learning,
Some because they have nothing better to do
Or because they hope these walls of books will deaden
    The drumming of the demon in their ears.

Cranks, hacks, poverty-stricken scholars,
In pince-nez, period hats or romantic beards
    And cherishing their hobby or their doom
Some are too much alive and some are asleep
Hanging like bats in a world of inverted values,
Folded up in themselves in a world which is safe and silent:
    This is the British Museum Reading Room.

[1] An early system of Physical Training.

Out on the steps in the sun the pigeons are courting,
Puffing their ruffs and sweeping their tails or taking
    A sun-bath at their ease
And under the totem poles — the ancient terror —
Between the enormous fluted Ionic columns
There seeps from heavily jowled or hawk-like foreign faces
    The guttural sorrow of the refugees.

Louis Macneice

Passage Steamer

Upon the decks they take beef tea
    Who are so free, so free, so free,
But down the ladder in the engine-room
    (Doom, doom, doom, doom)
The great cranks rise and fall, repeat,
The great cranks plod with their Assyrian feet
    To match the monotonous energy of the sea.

Back from a journey I require
    Some new desire, desire, desire
But find in the open sea and sun
    None, none, none, none;
The gulls that bank around the mast
Insinuate that nothing we pass is past,
    That all our beginnings were long since begun.

And when I think of you, my dear,
    Who were so near, so near, so near,
The barren skies from wall to wall
    Appal, appal, pall, pall,

28

The spray no longer gilds the wave,
The sea looks nothing more nor less than a grave
   And the world and the day are grey and that is all.

Louis Macneice

Turf-stacks

Among these turf-stacks graze no iron horses
Such as stalk, such as champ in towns and the soul of crowds,
Here is no mass-production of neat thoughts
No canvas shrouds for the mind nor any black hearses:
The peasant shambles on his boots like hooves
Without thinking at all or wanting to run in grooves.

But those who lack the peasant's conspirators,
The tawny mountain, the unregarded buttress,
Will feel the need of a fortress against ideas and against the
Shuddering insidious shock of the theory-vendors,
The little sardine men crammed in a monster toy
Who tilt their aggregate beast against our crumbling Troy.

For we are obsolete who like the lesser things
Who play in corners with looking-glasses and beads;
It is better we should go quickly, go into Asia
Or any other tunnel where the world recedes,
Or turn blind wantons like the gulls who scream
And rip the edge off any ideal or dream.

Louis Macneice

The Cyclist

Freewheeling down the escarpment past the unpassing horse
Blazoned in chalk the wind he causes in passing
Cools the sweat of his neck, making him one with the sky,
In the heat of the handlebars he grasps the summer
Being a boy and to-day a parenthesis
Between the horizon's brackets; the main sentence
Is to be picked up later but these five minutes
Are all to-day and summer. The dragonfly
Rises without take-off, horizontal,
Underlining itself in a sliver of peacock light.

And glaring, glaring white
The horse on the down moves within his brackets,
The grass boils with grasshoppers, a pebble
Scutters from under the wheel and all this country
Is spattered white with boys riding their heat-wave,
Feet on a narrow plank and hair thrown back

And a surf of dust beneath them. Summer, summer —
They chase it with butterfly nets or strike it into the deep
In a little red ball or gulp it lathered with cream
Or drink it through closed eyelids; until the bell
Left-right-left gives his forgotten sentence
And reaching the valley the boy must pedal again
Left-right-left but meanwhile
For ten seconds more can move as the horse in the chalk
Moves unbeginningly calmly
Calmly regardless of tenses and final clauses
Calmly unendingly moves.

Louis Macneice

30

Swing-song

I'm only a wartime working girl,
The machine shop makes me deaf.
I have no prospects after the war
And *my* young man is in the R.A.F.
        K for Kitty calling P for Prue ...
        Bomb Doors Open ...
        Over to You.

Night after night as he passes by
I wonder what he's gone to bomb
And I fancy in the jabber of the mad machines
That I hear him talking on the intercomm.
        K for Kitty calling P for Prue ...
        Bomb Doors Open ...
        Over to You.

So there's no one in the world, I sometimes think,
Such a wall flower as I
For I must talk to myself on the ground
While he is talking to his friends in the sky:
        K for Kitty calling P for Prue ...
        Bomb Doors Open ...
        Over to You.

Louis Macneice

Jigsaw II

Property! Property! Let us extend
Soul and body without end:
A box to live in, with airs and graces,
A box on wheels that shows its paces,
A box that talks or that makes faces,
And curtains and fences as good as the neighbours'
To keep out the neighbours and keep us immured
Enjoying the cold canned fruit of our labours
In a sterilized cell, unshared, insured.

Property! Property! When will it end?
When will the Poltergeist ascend
Out of the sewer with chopper and squib
To burn the mink and the baby's bib
And cut the tattling wire to town
And smash all the plastics, clowning and clouting,
And stop all the boxes shouting and pouting
And wreck the house from the aerial down
And give these ingrown souls an outing?

Louis Macneice

Extract *from* Autumn Journal

A week to Christmas, cards of snow and holly,
    Gimcracks in the shops,
Wishes and memories wrapped in tissue paper,
    Trinkets, gadgets and lollipops

And as if through coloured glasses
   We remember our childhood's thrill
Waking in the morning to the rustling of paper,
   The eiderdown heaped in a hill
Of wogs and dogs and bears and bricks and apples
   And the feeling that Christmas Day
Was a coral island in time where we land and eat our lotus
   But where we can never stay.
There was a star in the East, the magi in their turbans
   Brought their luxury toys
In homage to a child born to capsize their values
   And wreck their equipoise.
A smell of hay like peace in the dark stable —
   Not peace however but a sword
To cut the Gordian knot of logical self-interest,
   The fool-proof golden cord;
For Christ walked in where no philosopher treads
   But armed with more than folly,
Making the smooth place rough and knocking the heads
   Of Church and State together.
In honour of whom we have taken over the pagan
   Saturnalia for our annual treat
Letting the belly have its say, ignoring
   The spirit while we eat.
And Conscience still goes crying through the desert
   With sackcloth round his loins:
A week to Christmas — hark the herald angels
   Beg for copper coins.

Louis Macneice

Conclusion from Autumn Journal

What is it we want really?
  For what end and how?
If it is something feasible, obtainable,
  Let us dream it now,
And pray for a possible land
  Not of sleep-walkers, not of angry puppets,
But where both heart and brain can understand
  The movements of our fellows;
Where life is a choice of instruments and none
  Is debarred his natural music,
Where the waters of life are free of the ice-blockade of hunger
  And thought is free as the sun,
Where the altars of sheer power and mere profit
  Have fallen to disuse,
Where nobody sees the use
  Of buying money and blood at the cost of blood and money
Where the individual, no longer squandered
  In self-assertion, works with the rest, endowed
With the split vision of a juggler and the quick lock of a taxi,
  Where the people are more than a crowd.
So sleep in hope of this — but only for a little;
  Your hope must wake
While the choice is yours to make,
  The mortgage not foreclosed, the offer open.
Sleep serene, avoid the backward
  Glance; go forward, dreams, and do not halt
(Behind you in the desert stands a token
  Of doubt — a pillar of salt).[1]

[1] *Genesis*, XIX, 26.

Sleep, the past, and wake, the future,
    And walk out promptly through the open door;
But you, my coward doubts, may go on sleeping,
    You need not wake again — not any more.
The New Year comes with bombs, it is too late
    To dose the dead with honourable intentions:
If you have honour to spare, employ it on the living:
    The dead are dead as Nineteen-Thirty-Eight.
Sleep to the noise of running water
    To-morrow to be crossed, however deep;
This is no river of the dead or Lethe,
    To-night we sleep
On the banks of Rubicon — the die is cast;
    There will be time to audit
The accounts later, there will be sunlight later
    And the equation will come out at last.

Louis Macneice

*   *   *

Despite being officially listed as 'Died of Wounds' during the First World War, Robert Graves, at his home in Majorca, continues to write poetry, novels and essays in great abundance.

A full account of his 'death' is given in his autobiography Goodbye To All That.

1805

At Viscount Nelson's lavish funeral,
    While the mob milled and yelled about St. Paul's,
A General chatted with an Admiral:

'One of your Colleagues, Sir, remarked to-day
    That Nelson's *exit*, though to be lamented,
Falls not inopportunely, in its way.'

'He was a thorn in our flesh,' came the reply —
    'The most bird-witted, unaccountable,
Odd little runt that ever I did spy.

'One arm, one peeper, vain as Pretty Poll,
    A meddler, too, in foreign politics
And gave his heart in pawn to a plain moll.

'He would dare lecture us Sea Lords, and then
    Would treat his ratings as though men of honour
And play at leap-frog with his midshipmen:

'We tried to box him down, but up he popped,
    And when he'd banged Napoleon at the Nile
Became too much the hero to be dropped.

'You've heard that Copenhagen "blind eye" story?
    We'd tied him to Nurse Parker's apron-strings —
By G—d, he snipped them through and snatched the glory!'

'Yet,' cried the General, 'six-and-twenty-sail
    Captured or sunk by him off Trafalgar —
That writes a handsome *finis* to the tale.'

'Handsome enough. The seas are England's now.
    That fellow's foibles need no longer plague us.
He died most creditably, I'll allow.'

'And, Sir, the secret of his victories?'
  'By his unServicelike, familiar ways, Sir,
He made the whole Fleet love him, damn his eyes!'

Robert Graves

'The General Elliott'

He fell in victory's fierce pursuit,
  Holed through and through with shot;
A sabre sweep had hacked him deep
  'Twixt neck and shoulder-knot.

The potman cannot well recall,
  The ostler never knew,
Whether that day was Malplaquet,
  The Boyne, or Waterloo.

But there he hangs, a tavern sign,
  With foolish bold regard
For cock and hen and loitering men
  And wagons down the yard.

Raised high above the hayseed world
  He smokes his china pipe;
And now surveys the orchard ways,
  The damsons clustering ripe —

Stares at the churchyard slabs beyond,
  Where country neighbours lie:
Their brief renown set lowly down,
  But his invades the sky.

He grips a tankard of brown ale
  That spills a generous foam:
Often he drinks, they say, and winks
  At drunk men lurching home.

No upstart hero may usurp
  That honoured swinging seat;
His seasons pass with pipe and glass
  Until the tale's complete —

And paint shall keep his buttons bright
  Though all the world's forgot
Whether he died for England's pride
  By battle or by pot.

Robert Graves

Lollocks

By sloth on sorrow fathered,
These dusty-featured Lollocks
Have their nativity in all disordered
Backs of cupboard drawers.

They play hide and seek
Among collars and novels
And empty medicine bottles,
And letters from abroad
That never will be answered.

Every sultry night
They plague little children,
Gurgling from the cistern,

Humming from the air,
Skewing up the bed-clothes,
Twitching the blind.

When the imbecile agèd
Are over-long in dying
And the nurse drowses,
Lollocks come skipping
Up the tattered stairs
And are nasty together
In the bed's shadow.

The signs of their presence
Are boils on the neck,
Dreams of vexation suddenly recalled
In the middle of the morning,
Languor after food.

Men cannot see them,
Men cannot hear them,
Do not believe in them –
But suffer the more,
Both in neck and belly.

Women can see them –
O those naughty wives
Who sit by the fireside
Munching bread and honey,
Watching them in mischief
From corners of their eyes,
Slyly allowing them to lick
Honey-sticky fingers.

Sovereign against Lollocks
Are hard broom and soft broom,
To well comb the hair,
To well brush the shoe,
And to pay every debt
So soon as it's due.

Robert Graves

Warning to Children

Children, if you dare to think
Of the greatness, rareness, muchness,
Fewness of this precious only
Endless world in which you say
You live, you think of things like this:
Blocks of slate enclosing dappled
Red and green, enclosing tawny
Yellow nets, enclosing white
And black acres of dominoes,
Where a neat brown paper parcel
Tempts you to untie the string.
In the parcel a small island,
On the island a large tree,
On the tree a husky fruit.
Strip the husk and pare the rind off:
In the centre you will see
Blocks of slate enclosed by dappled
Red and green, enclosed by tawny
Yellow nets, enclosed by white
And black acres of dominoes,
Where the same brown paper parcel —
Children, leave the string untied!

For who dares undo the parcel
Finds himself at once inside it,
On the island, in the fruit,
Blocks of slate about his head,
Finds himself enclosed by dappled
Green and red, enclosed by yellow
Tawny nets, enclosed by black
And white acres of dominoes,
With the same brown paper parcel
Still untied upon his knee.
And, if he then should dare to think
Of the fewness, muchness, rareness,
Greatness of this endless only
Precious world in which he says
He lives — he then unties the string.

Robert Graves

'¡*Wellcome to the Caves of Arta*!'

Guide-books and leaflets produced in foreign countries for English-speaking tourists are occasionally 'eccentric' in their spelling, punctuation and grammar, as the printed extract shows. Robert Graves found the possibilities of this new language irresistible and this poem is the result.

'They are hollowed out in the see coast at the muncipal terminal of Capdepera, at nine kilometer from the town of Arta in the Island of Mallorca, with a suporizing infinity of graceful colums of 21 meter and by downward, wich prives the spectator of all animacion and plunges in dumbness. The way going is very picturesque, serpentine between style mountains, til the arrival at the esplanade of

the vallee called "The Spider". There are good enlacements of the
railroad with autobuses of excursion, many days of the week, today
actually Wednesday and Saturday. Since many centuries renown
foreing visitors have explored them and wrote their eulogy about,
included Nort-American geoglogues.'

(*From a Tourist leaflet*)

Such subtile filigranity and nobless of construccion
   Here fraternise in harmony, that respiracion stops.
While all admit thier impotence (though autors most formidable)
To sing in words the excellence of Nature's underprops,
Yet stalactite and stalagmite together with dumb language
Make hymnes to God wich celebrate the stregnth of water drops.

  You, also, are you capable to make precise in idiom
Consideracions magic of ilusions very wide?
Alraedy in the Vestibule of these Grand Caves of Arta
The spirit of the human verb is darked and stupefyed;
So humildy you trespass trough the forest of the colums
And listen to the grandess explicated by the guide.

From darkness into darkness, but at measure, now descending
You remark with what esxactitude he designates each bent;
'The Saloon of Thousand Banners', or 'The Tumba of Napoleon',
'The Grotto of the Rosary', 'The Club', 'The Camping Tent'.
And at 'Cavern of the Organ' there are knocking streange
   formacions
Wich give a nois particular pervoking wonderment.

  Too far do not adventure, sir! For, further as you wander,
The every of the stalactites will make you stop and stay.
Grand peril amenaces now, your nostrills aprehending

An odour least delicious of lamentable decay.
It is some poor touristers, in the depth of obscure cristal,
Wich deceased of thier emocion on a past excursion day.

Robert Graves

Traveller's Curse after Misdirection

(from the Welsh)

> May they stumble, stage by stage
> On an endless pilgrimage,
> Dawn and dusk, mile after mile,
> At each and every step, a stile;
> At each and every step withal
> May they catch their feet and fall;
> At each and every fall they take
> May a bone within them break;
> And may the bone that breaks within
> Not be, for variation's sake,
> Now rib, now thigh, now arm, now shin,
> But always, without fail THE NECK.

Robert Graves

Flying Crooked

> The butterfly, a cabbage-white,
> (His honest idiocy of flight)
> Will never now, it is too late,
> Master the art of flying straight,
> Yet has — who knows so well as I? —
> A just sense of how not to fly:

43

He lurches here and here by guess
And God and hope and hopelessness.
Even the aerobatic swift,
Has not his flying-crooked gift.

Robert Graves

*   *   *

Though decorated with the Military Cross during the First World War, Siegfried Sassoon grew to hate the horror and carnage of war and publicly protested against its continuation (see Memoirs of an Infantry Officer). In the post-war period he often felt that, far from learning of the futility of war, mankind was preparing for a second conflict. This feeling is behind the next two poems.

At the Cenotaph

I saw the Prince of Darkness, with his Staff,
Standing bare-headed by the Cenotaph:
Unostentatious and respectful, there
He stood, and offered up the following prayer.
  'Make them forget, O Lord, what this Memorial
    Means; their discredited ideas revive;
  Breed new belief that War is purgatorial
    Proof of the pride and power of being alive;
  Men's biologic urge to readjust
    The Map of Europe, Lord of Hosts, increase;
  Lift up their hearts in large destructive lust;
    And crown their heads with blind vindictive Peace.'
The Prince of Darkness to the Cenotaph
Bowed. As he walked away I heard him laugh.

Siegfried Sassoon

Thoughts in 1932

Alive — and forty-five — I jogged my way
Across a dull green day,
Listening to larks and plovers, well content
With the pre-Roman pack-road where I went.

Pastoral and pleasant was the end of May.
But readers of the times had cause to say
That skies were brighter for the late Victorians;
And 'The Black Thirties' seemed a sobriquet
Likely to head the chapters of historians.

Above Stonehenge a drone of engines drew
My gaze; there seven and twenty war-planes flew
Manœuvring in formation; and the drone
Of that neat-patterned hornet-gang was thrown
Across the golden downland like a blight.

Cities, I thought, will wait them in the night
When airmen, with high-minded motives, fight
To save Futurity. In years to come
Poor panic-stricken hordes will hear that hum,
And Fear will be synonymous with Flight.

Siegfried Sassoon

The Case for the Miners

The survivors of the war of 1914–18 were promised 'a land fit for heroes' but found that the early years of peace were ones of industrial unrest. Here Sassoon, whose sympathies with the working man had been developed through his war-time experiences, finds himself alone when trying to defend the miners during their strike for better conditions and wages.

Something goes wrong with my synthetic brain
When I defend the Strikers and explain
My reasons for not blackguarding the Miners.
'*What do you know?*' exclaim my fellow-diners
(Peeling their plovers' eggs or lifting glasses
Of mellowed *Château Rentier* from the table),
'*What do you know about the working classes?*'

I strive to hold my own; but I'm unable
To state the case succinctly. Indistinctly
I mumble about World-Emancipation,
Standards of Living, Nationalization
Of Industry; until they get me tangled
In superficial details; goad me on
To unconvincing vagueness. When we've wrangled
From soup to savoury, my temper's gone.

'*Why should a miner earn six pounds a week?*
Leisure! They'd only spend it in a bar!
Standard of life! You'll never teach them Greek,
Or make them more contented than they are!'
That's how my port-flushed friends discuss the Strike.
And that's the reason why I shout and splutter.
And that's the reason why I'd almost like
To see them hawking matches in the gutter.

Siegfried Sassoon

To a Conscript of 1940

Qui n'a pas une fois désespéré de l'honneur, ne sera jamais un héros.[1]

GEORGES BERNANOS

A soldier passed me in the freshly fallen snow
His footsteps muffled, his face unearthly grey;
And my heart gave a sudden leap
As I gazed on a ghost of five-and-twenty years ago.

I shouted Halt! and my voice had the old accustom'd ring
And he obeyed it as it was obeyed
In the shrouded days when I too was one
Of an army of young men marching

Into the unknown. He turned towards me and I said:
'I am one of those who went before you
Five-and-twenty years ago: one of the many who never returned
Of the many who returned and yet were dead.

We went where you are going, into the rain and the mud;
We fought as you will fight
With death and darkness and despair;
We gave what you will give — our brains and our blood.

We think we gave in vain. The world was not renewed.
There was hope in the homestead and anger in the streets
But the old world was restored and we returned
To the dreary field and workshop, and the immemorial feud

---

[1] He who has not at some time given up hope of honour will never be a hero.

Of rich and poor. Our victory was our defeat.
Power was retained where power had been misused
And youth was left to sweep away
The ashes that the fires had strewn beneath our feet.

But one thing we learned: there is no glory in the deed
Until the soldier wears a badge of tarnish'd braid;
There are heroes who have heard the rally and have seen
The glitter of a garland round their head.

Theirs is the hollow victory. They are deceived.
But you, my brother and my ghost, if you can go
Knowing that there is no reward, no certain use
In all your sacrifice, then honour is reprieved.

To fight without hope is to fight with grace,
The self reconstructed, the false heart repaired,
Then I turned with a smile, and he answered my salute
As he stood against the fretted hedge, which was like white lace.

Herbert Read

The Ivy and the Ash

The ivy and the ash
cast a dark arm
across the beck.
In this rocky ghyll
I sit and watch
the eye-iris water move
like muscles over stones
smooth'd by this ageless action.

48

The water brings
from the high fell
an icy current of air.
There is no sun to splinter
the grey visionary quartz.
The heart is cool
and adamant among the rocks
mottled with wet moss.

Descend into the valley
explore the plain
even the salt sea
but keep the heart
cool in the memory
of ivy, ash
and the glistening beck
running swiftly through the black rocks.

Herbert Read

Night Ride

Along the black
leather strap
of the night
deserted road

swiftly rolls
the freighted bus.
Huddled together
two lovers doze

their hands linkt
across their laps
their bodies loosely
interlockt

their heads resting
two heavy fruits
on the plaited
basket of their limbs.

Slowly the bus
slides into light.
Here are hills
detach'd from dark

the road, uncoils
a white ribbon
the lovers with
the hills unfold

wake cold
to face the fate
of those who love
despite the world.

Herbert Read

The Castle

All through that summer at ease we lay,
And daily from the turret wall
We watched the mowers in the hay
And the enemy half a mile away.
They seemed no threat to us at all.

For what, we thought, had we to fear
With our arms and provender, load on load,
Our towering battlements, tier on tier,
And friendly allies drawing near
On every leafy summer road.

Our gates were strong, our walls were thick,
So smooth and high, no man could win
A foothold there, no clever trick
Could take us, have us dead or quick.
Only a bird could have got in.

What could they offer us for bait?
Our captain was brave and we were true ...
There was a little private gate,
A little wicked wicket gate.
The wizened warder let them through.

Oh then our maze of tunnelled stone
Grew thin and treacherous as air.
The cause was lost without a groan,
The famous citadel overthrown,
And all its secret galleries bare.

How can this shameful tale be told?
I will maintain until my death
We could do nothing, being sold;
Our only enemy was gold,
And we had no arms to fight it with.

Edwin Muir

Suburban Dream

Walking the suburbs in the afternoon
In summer when the idle doors stand open
   And the air flows through the rooms
   Fanning the curtain hems,

You wander through a cool elysium
Of women, schoolgirls, children, garden talks,
   With a schoolboy here and there
   Conning his history book.

The men are all away in offices,
Committee-rooms, laboratories, banks,
   Or pushing cotton goods
   In Wick or Ilfracombe.

The massed unanimous absence liberates
The light keys of the piano and sets free
   Chopin and everlasting youth,
   Now, with the masters gone.

And all things turn to images of peace,
The boy curled over his book, the young girl poised
   On the path as if beguiled
   By the silence of a wood.

It is a child's dream of a grown-up world.
But soon the brazen evening clocks will bring
   The tramp of feet and brisk
   Fanfare of motor horns
   And the masters come.

The Killing

That was the day they killed the Son of God
On a squat hill-top by Jerusalem.
Zion was bare, her children from their maze
Sucked by the demon curiosity
Clean through the gates. The very halt and blind
Had somehow got themselves up to the hill.

After the ceremonial preparation,
The scourging, nailing, nailing against the wood,
Erection of the main-trees with their burden,
While from the hill rose an orchestral wailing,
They were there at last, high up in the soft spring day.
We watched the writhings, heard the moanings, saw
The three heads turning on their separate axles
Like broken wheels left spinning. Round *his* head
Was loosely bound a crown of plaited thorn
That hurt at random, stinging temple and brow
As the pain swung into its envious circle.
In front the wreath was gathered in a knot
That as he gazed looked like the last stump left
Of a death-wounded deer's great antlers. Some
Who came to stare grew silent as they looked,
Indignant or sorry. But the hardened old
And the hard-hearted young, although at odds
From the first morning, cursed him with one curse,
Having prayed for a Rabbi or an armed Messiah
And found the Son of God. What use to them
Was a God or a Son of God? Of what avail
For purposes such as theirs? Beside the cross-foot,
Alone, four women stood and did not move

All day. The sun revolved, the shadow wheeled,
The evening fell. His head lay on his breast,
But in his breast they watched his heart move on
By itself alone, accomplishing its journey.
Their taunts grew louder, sharpened by the knowledge
That he was walking in the park of death,
Far from their rage. Yet all grew stale at last,
Spite, curiosity, envy, hate itself.
They waited only for death and death was slow
And came so quietly they scarce could mark it.
They were angry then with death and death's deceit.

I was a stranger, could not read these people
Or this outlandish deity. Did a God
Indeed in dying cross my life that day
By chance, he on his road and I on mine?

Edwin Muir

Mountain Lion

Climbing through the January snow, into the Lobo canyon
Dark grow the spruce-trees, blue is the balsam, water sounds
  still unfrozen, and the trail is still evident.

Men!
Two men!
Men! The only animal in the world to fear!

They hesitate.
We hesitate.
They have a gun.
We have no gun.

Then we all advance, to meet.

54

Two Mexicans, strangers, emerging out of the dark
    and snow and inwardness of the Lobo valley.
What are you doing here on this vanishing trail?

What is he carrying?
Something yellow.
A deer?

Qué tiene, amigo?[1]

León —

He smiles, foolishly, as if he were caught doing wrong.
And we smile, foolishly, as if we didn't know.
He is quite gentle and dark-faced.

It is a mountain lion,
A long, long slim cat, yellow like a lioness.
Dead.
He trapped her this morning, he says, smiling foolishly.

Lift up her face,
Her round bright face, bright as frost.
Her round, fine-fashioned head, with two dead ears;
And stripes in the brilliant frost of her face, sharp, fine dark rays,
Dark, keen fine eyes in the brilliant frost of her face.
Beautiful dead eyes.

Hermoso es![2]

They go out towards the open;
We go on into the gloom of Lobo.
And above the trees I found her lair,

[1] What have you there, my friend?   [2] It is beautiful.

A hole in the blood-orange brilliant rocks that stick up, a little
    cave.
And bones, and twigs, and a perilous ascent.

So, she will never leap up that way again, with the yellow flash
    of a mountain lion's long shoot!
And her bright striped frost-face will never watch any more,
    out of the shadow of the cave in the blood-orange rock,
Above the trees of the Lobo dark valley-mouth!
Instead, I look out.
And out to the dim of the desert, like a dream, never real;

To the snow of the Sangre de Cristo mountains, the ice of the
    mountains of Picoris,
And near across at the opposite steep of snow, green trees
    motionless standing in snow, like a Christmas toy.

And I think in this empty world there was room for me and a
    mountain lion.
And I think in the world beyond, how easily we might spare a
    million or two of humans
And never miss them.
Yet what a gap in the world, the missing white frost-face of that
    slim yellow mountain lion!

Lobo
D. H. Lawrence

H.M.S. Hero

The Tyne has long been famous for its shipyards, and vessels for the Royal Navy have been constructed there for many generations.

Pale grey, her guns hooded, decks clear of all impediment,
Easily, between the swart tugs, she glides in the pale October
    sunshine:
It is Saturday afternoon, and the men are at football,
The wharves and the cobbled streets are silent by the slow river.

Smoothly, rounding the long bend, she glides to her place in
    history,
Past the grimed windows cracked and broken,
Past Swan Hunter's, Hawthorn Leslie's, Armstrong's,
Down to the North Sea, and trials, and her first commission.

Here is grace; and a job well done; built only for one end.
Women watch from the narrow doorways and give no sign,
Children stop playing by the wall and stare in silence
At gulls wheeling above the Tyne, or the ship passing.

Michael Roberts

La Meije 1937

For Ottone Bron: killed on the Col du Géant, 1938

Michael Roberts was a devoted climber and Ottone Bron, who later become a close friend, was the guide who accompanied him on his first big climbs. Bron was killed while climbing the Glacier du Géant when a snow bridge collapsed underneath him. Bron's motto was, 'Il faut toujours faire le plus difficile' — 'Always do the most difficult'.

Going down from the Aiguilles d'Arves, toward la Grave,
With sunlight on the cornsheaves, and the evening voices,
The fields already ripe with autumn crocus,
We said nothing, but saw the Meije rise up across the valley.

That was a climb for the next day, or the next;
That was our country, there, high up,
A world barely older than ourselves, and none too easy;
But now we were going down to the valley,
Going down among the hotels and autocars,
Going down among the young men in flannels, and the fat
    mammas,
Sightseers like ourselves, but easily contented,
Speaking more kindly of us than we of them.

This was our pleasure: to climb among loose stones, to cut steps
    in ice,
To find a new alternative to the *mauvais pas*;[1]
Theirs was simpler, and we despised it.
Perhaps we were right:
A man should use every nerve and muscle,
A man should puzzle out the hardest questions,
A man should find words for the thoughts that no one knows.
At any rate, there was no room for us at the big hotel.

But the fields were filled with sunlight,
We clattered noisily through the upper hamlets,
Girls turned for a moment from the milking,
Old men smiled from the stone doorways,
And a boy with six goats shouted a greeting,
To us, the intruders.

Michael Roberts

[1] A dangerous situation; a 'fix' or 'jam'.

The Images of Death

Here Roberts seems to be adopting Bron's motto (see previous note) as the guiding principle in his own life.

The hawk, the furred eagle, the smooth panther —
Images of desire and power, images of death,
These we adore and fear, these we need,
Move in the solitude of night or the tall sky,
Move with a strict grace to the one fulfilment:
The Greenland falcon, the beautiful one,
Lives on carrion and dives inevitably to the prey.

To be human is more difficult:
To be human is to know oneself, to hold the broken mirror,
To become aware of justice, truth, mercy,
To choose the difficult road, to aim
Crookedly, for the direct aim is failure,
To abandon the way of the hawk and the grey falcon.

These fall, and fall stupidly:
To be human is to fall, but not stupidly;
To suffer, but not for a simple end;
To choose, and know the penalty of choice;
To read the intensity of human eyes and features;
To know the intricacy of life and the value of death;
To remember the furred eagle and the smooth panther,
The images of death, and death's simplicity.

Michael Roberts

'Already', said my host

Roberts died in 1948 at the early age of forty-six and this poem was written during his last illness.

'Already', said my host. 'You have arrived already?
But by what route, what ingenious *raccourci*?[1]
I half-expected you, it is true,
But I expected someone a little older,
Someone rather less arrogant and impulsive,
Someone a little embittered and despondent,
Someone, in short, not quite *you*.
And now you arrive by some unfair expedient,
Having neglected, no doubt, to pay proper attention to the view:
You arrive a little dazed and flushed,
And you find me hardly ready to receive you, hardly able to
    cope.
It was inconsiderate of you to die so suddenly,
Placing me in this ridiculous quandary.
I had predicted a great future for you,
A future without happiness or hope;
I had prepared a suitable mausoleum for your reception:
And now you arrive with a bundle of daffodils, a fox-terrier,
And a still unfinished smile.
Really!'

Michael Roberts

And death shall have no dominion

The Welsh are extremely sensitive to the power of words and music to arouse and express intense emotion. Dylan Thomas was no exception. His language is vivid, passionate and occasionally

[1] A short cut.

*mysterious, so that there are times when his poetry sounds like the
weaving of spells or the uttering of incantations.*

And death shall have no dominion.
Dead men naked they shall be one
With the man in the wind and the west moon;
When their bones are picked clean and the clean bones gone,
They shall have stars at elbow and foot;
Though they go mad they shall be sane,
Though they sink through the sea they shall rise again;
Though lovers be lost love shall not;
And death shall have no dominion.

And death shall have no dominion.
Under the windings of the sea
They lying long shall not die windily;
Twisting on racks when sinews give way,
Strapped to a wheel, yet they shall not break;
Faith in their hands shall snap in two,
And the unicorn evils run them through;
Split all ends up they shan't crack;
And death shall have no dominion.

And death shall have no dominion.
No more may gulls cry at their ears
Or waves break loud on the seashores;
Where blew a flower may a flower no more
Lift its head to the blows of the rain;
Though they be mad and dead as nails,
Heads of the characters hammer through daisies;
Break in the sun till the sun breaks down,
And death shall have no dominion.

Dylan Thomas

The hand that signed the paper

The hand that signed the paper felled a city;
Five sovereign fingers taxed the breath,
Doubled the globe of dead and halved a country;
These five kings did a king to death.

The mighty hand leads to a sloping shoulder,
The fingers joints are cramped with chalk;
A goose's quill has put an end to murder
That put an end to talk.

The hand that signed the treaty bred a fever,
And famine grew, and locusts came;
Great is the hand that holds dominion over
Man by a scribbled name.

The five kings count the dead but do not soften
The crusted wound nor stroke the brow;
A hand rules pity as a hand rules heaven;
Hands have no tears to flow.

Dylan Thomas

Poem in October

It was my thirtieth year to heaven
Woke to my hearing from harbour and neighbour wood
And the mussel pooled and the heron
Priested shore
The morning beckon
With water praying and call of seagull and rook
And the knock of sailing boats on the net webbed wall

Myself to set foot
That second
In the still sleeping town and set forth.

My birthday began with the water—
Birds and the birds of the winged trees flying my name
Above the farms and the white horses
And I rose
In rainy autumn
And walked abroad in a shower of all my days.
High tide and the heron dived when I took the road
Over the border
And the gates
Of the town closed as the town awoke.

A springful of larks in a rolling
Cloud and the roadside bushes brimming with whistling
Blackbirds and the sun of October
Summery
On the hill's shoulder,
Here were fond climates and sweet singers suddenly
Come in the morning where I wandered and listened
To the rain wringing
Wind blow cold
In the wood faraway under me.

Pale rain over the dwindling harbour
And over the sea-wet church the size of a snail
With its horns through mist and the castle
Brown as owls
But all the gardens
Of spring and summer were blooming in the tall tales
Beyond the border and under the lark full cloud.

63

There could I marvel
My birthday
Away but the weather turned around. *changed*

It turned away from the blithe country *gay*
And down the other air and the blue altered sky
Streamed again a wonder of summer *rays of sun*
With apples
Pears and red currants
And I saw in the turning so clearly a child's
Forgotten mornings when he walked with his mother
Through the parables
Of sun light
And the legends of the green chapels

And the twice told fields of infancy
That his tears burned my cheeks and his heart moved in mine.
These were the woods the river and sea
Where a boy
In the listening
Summertime of the dead whispered the truth of his joy
To the trees and the stones and the fish in the tide.
And the mystery
Sang alive
Still in the water and singingbirds.

And there could I marvel my birthday
Away but the weather turned around. And the true
Joy of the long dead child sang burning
In the sun.
It was my thirtieth
Year to heaven stood there then in the summer noon
Though the town below lay leaved with October blood.

O may my heart's truth
    still be sung
On this high hill in a year's turning.

Dylan Thomas

The Hunchback in the Park

The hunchback in the park
A solitary mister
Propped between trees and water
From the opening of the garden lock
That lets the trees and water enter
Until the Sunday sombre bell at dark

Eating bread from a newspaper
Drinking water from the chained cup
That the children filled with gravel
In the fountain basin where I sailed my ship
Slept at night in a dog kennel
But nobody chained him up.

Like the park birds he came early
Like the water he sat down
And Mister they called Hey mister
The truant boys from the town
Running when he had heard them clearly
On out of sound

Past lake and rockery
Laughing when he shook his paper
Hunchbacked in mockery
Through the loud zoo of the willow groves
Dodging the park keeper
With his stick that picked up leaves.

And the old dog sleeper
Alone between nurses and swans
While the boys among willows
Made the tigers jump out of their eyes
To roar on the rockery stones
And the groves were blue with sailors

Made all day until bell time
A woman figure without fault
Straight as a young elm
Straight and tall from his crooked bones
That she might stand in the night
After the locks and chains

All night in the unmade park
After the railings and shrubberies
The birds the grass the trees the lake
And the wild boys innocent as strawberries
Had followed the hunchback
To his kennel in the dark.

Dylan Thomas

Beauty never visits mining places

Beauty never visits mining places,
For the yellow smoke taints the summer air.
Despair graves lines on the dwellers' faces,
My fellows' faces, for my fellows live there.

There by the wayside dusty weed drowses,
The darnel and dock and starwort run rife;
Gaunt folk stare from the doors of houses,
Folk with no share in the beauty of life.

66

There on slag heaps, where no bird poises,
My fellows' wan children tumble and climb,
Playing in the dust, making shrill noises,
Sweet human flowers that will fall ere their time.

Playing in the slag with their white faces,
Where headstocks loom by the railway lines —
Round-eyed children cheated of life's graces —
My fellows' children, born for the mines.

F. C. Boden

Nay, there's neither hope nor ease

Nay, there's neither hope nor ease,
And I'll be a bitter thing,
And I'll make what songs I please,
     And I will sing.

Bitter as my songs may be,
Who can bid his tongue be still?
Singing's all that's left for me,
     And sing I will.

Who lies down no more to range?
Who retreats afraid of life?
Strife's the father of all change:
     I sing of strife.

I'll not sit as still as stone,
And watch unmoved my fellows' wrongs,
Strife I sing and strife alone,
     And here's my songs.

F. C. Boden

As I came home from labour

As I came home from labour,
So stiff with sweat and pain,
I heard two starlings singing
Above the long pit-lane.

Their songs were all of summer,
And hope and love lives yet;
But I was sick and weary
And stiff with pain and sweat.

They sing, thought I, of pleasure,
And pain is never done;
They sing of ease and comfort,
And comfort I have none.

There's naught for folk who labour
But misery and rue;
No ease is theirs, no solace,
No hope the whole world thro'.

And there I lingered grieving,
And heard those happy songs,
And thought of all who labour
And bear their bitter wrongs.

F. C. Boden

The Pike

From shadows of rich oaks outpeer
The moss-green bastions of the weir,
Where the quick dipper forages
In elver-peopled crevices,
And a small runlet trickling down the sluice
Gossamer music tires not to unloose.

Else round the broad pool's hush
     Nothing stirs,
Unless sometimes a straggling heifer crush
Through the thronged spinney where the pheasant whirs
     Or martins in a flash
Come with wild mirth to dip their magical wings,
While in the shallow some doomed bulrush swings
At whose hid root the diver vole's teeth gnash.

And nigh this toppling reed, still as the dead
     The great pike lies, the murderous patriarch
     Watching the waterpit sheer-shelving dark,
Where through the plash his lithe bright vassals thread.

The rose-finned roach and bluish bream
And staring ruffe steal up the stream
Hard by their glutted tyrant, now
Still as a sunken bough.

He on the sandbank lies,
     Sunning himself long hours
With stony gorgon eyes:
     Westward the hot sun lowers.

Sudden the gray pike changes, and quivering poises for slaughter;
      Intense terror wakens around him, the shoals scud
          awry, but there chances
      A chub unsuspecting; the prowling fins quicken, in
          fury he lances;
And the miller that opens the hatch stands amazed at the whirl
   in the water.

Edmund Blunden

All day it has rained

Alun Lewis was killed in Burma in 1942 while fighting with the South Wales Borderers against the Japanese. The following poem describes an encounter with another enemy — boredom.

All day it has rained, and we on the edge of the moors
Have sprawled in our bell-tents, moody and dull as boors,
Groundsheets and blankets spread on the muddy ground
And from the first grey wakening we have found
No refuge from the skirmishing fine rain
And the wind that made the canvas heave and flap
And the taut wet guy-ropes ravel out and snap.
All day the rain has glided, wave and mist and dream,
Drenching the gorse and heather, a gossamer stream
Too light to stir the acorns that suddenly
Snatched from their cups by the wild south-westerly
Pattered against the tent and our upturned dreaming faces.
And we stretched out, unbuttoning our braces,
Smoking a Woodbine, darning dirty socks,
Reading the Sunday papers — I saw a fox
And mentioned it in the note I scribbled home; —
And we talked of girls, and dropping bombs on Rome,

And thought of the quiet dead and the loud celebrities
Exhorting us to slaughter, and the herded refugees;
— Yet thought softly, morosely of them, and as indifferently
As of ourselves or those whom we
For years have loved, and will again
To-morrow maybe love; but now it is the rain
Possesses us entirely, the twilight and the rain.

And I can remember nothing dearer or more to my heart
Than the children I watched in the woods on Saturday
Shaking down burning chestnuts for the schoolyard's merry play
Or the shaggy patient dog who followed me
By Sheet and Steep and up the wooded scree
To the Shoulder o' Mutton where Edward Thomas[1] brooded
    long
On death and beauty — till a bullet stopped his song.

Alun Lewis

The Mountain over Aberdare

From this high quarried ledge I see
The place for which the Quakers once
Collected clothes, my fathers' home,
Our stubborn bankrupt village sprawled
In jaded dusk beneath its nameless hills;
The drab streets strung across the cwm,[2]
Derelict workings, tips of slag
The gospellers and gamblers use
And children scrutting for the coal
That winter dole cannot purvey;

[1] A poet killed in the First World War.
[2] Valley, vale or hollow. It is pronounced 'coom'.

Allotments where the collier digs
While engines hack the coal within his brain;
Grey Hebron in a rigid cramp,
White cheap-jack cinema, the church
Stretched like a sow beside the stream;
And mourners in their Sunday best
Holding a tiny funeral, singing hymns
That drift insidious as the rain
Which rises from the steaming fields
And swathes about the skyline crags
Till all the upland gorse is drenched
And all the creaking mountain gates
Drip brittle tears of crystal peace;
And in a curtained parlour women hug
Huge grief, and anger against God.

But now the dusk, more charitable than Quakers,
Veils the cracked cottages with drifting may
And rubs the hard day off the slate.
The colliers squatting on the ashtip
Listen to one who holds them still with tales,
While that white frock that floats down the dark alley
Looks just like Christ; and in the lane
The clink of coins among the gamblers
Suggests the thirty pieces of silver.

I watch the clouded years
Rune[1] the rough foreheads of these moody hills,
This wet evening, in a lost age.

Alun Lewis

[1] Runes are characters from the old Scandinavian alphabet. They were often cut into ancient Norse monuments.

Sacco Writes to his Son

Nicolo Sacco and Bartolomeo Vanzetti were arrested in 1920 in the United States on a charge of murder. After legal wranglings lasting seven years they were eventually executed, although another man had made a confession which seemed to exonerate these two poor Italian immigrants. In the opinion of many thousands of people inside and outside the United States, Sacco and Vanzetti were 'framed' because of their political beliefs. Below is an extract from the letter which Sacco, on the eve of his execution, wrote to his son Dante. This letter became widely known and provided the raw material for Alun Lewis's poem, Sacco Writes to his Son.

To his Son Dante

Well, my dear boy, after your mother had talked to me so much and I had dreamed of you day and night, how joyful it was to see you at last. To have talked with you like we used to in the days — in those days. Much I told you on that visit and more I wanted to say, but I saw that you will remain the same affectionate boy, faithful to your mother who loves you so much, and I did not want to hurt your sensibilities any longer, because I am sure that you will continue to be the same boy and remember what I have told you. I knew that and what here I am going to tell you will touch your sensibilities, but don't cry Dante, because many tears have been wasted, as your mother's have been wasted for seven years, and never did any good. So, Son, instead of crying, be strong, so as to be able to comfort your mother from the discouraging soulness, I will tell you what I used to do. To take her for a long walk in the quiet country, gathering wild flowers here and there, resting under the shade of trees, between the harmony of the vivid stream and the gentle tranquillity of the mothernature, and I am sure that she will enjoy this very much, as you surely would be happy for it. But remember always, Dante, in the

73

*play of happiness, don't you use all for yourself only, but down your-
self just one step, at your side and help the weak ones that cry for
help, help the prosecuted and the victim, because that are your better
friends; they are the comrades that fight and fall as your father and
Bartolo fought and fell yesterday for the conquest of the joy of freedom
for all and the poor workers. In this struggle of life you will find more
love and you will be loved.*

*P.S. Bartolo send you the most affectionate greetings. I hope that
your mother will help you to understand this letter because I could
have written much better and more simple, if I was feeling good. But
I am so weak.*

> I did not want to die. I wanted you,
> You and your sister Inez and your mother.
> Reject this death, my Dante, seek out Life,
> Yet not the death-in-life that most men live.
> My body aches ... I think I hear you weep.
> You must not weep. Tears are a waste of strength.
> Seven years your mother wept, not as your mother,
> But as my wife. So make her more your mother.
> Take her the ways I know she can escape
> From the poor soulness that so wearies her.
> Take her into the country every Sunday,
> Ask her the name of such and such a plant,
> Gather a basket each of herbs and flowers,
> Ask her to find the robin where he nests,
> She will be happy then. Tears do no damage
> That spring from gladness, though they scald the throat.
> Go patiently about it. Not too much
> Just yet, Dante, good boy. You'll know.

> And for yourself, remember in the play
> Of happiness you must not act alone.

74

The joy is in the sharing of the feast.
Also be like a man in how you greet
The suffering that makes your young face thin.
Be not perturbed if you are called to fight.
Only a fool thinks life was made his way,
A fool or the daughter of a wealthy house.
Husband yourself, but never stale your mind
With prudence or with doubting. I could wish
You saw my body slipping from the chair
To-morrow. You'd remember that, my son,
And would not weigh the cost of our struggle
Against the product as a poor wife does.
But I'll not break your sleep with such a nightmare.
You looked so happy when you lay asleep ...

But I have neither strength nor room for all
These thoughts. One single thought's enough
To fill immensity. I drop my pen ...

I hope this letter finds you in good health,
My son, my comrade. Will you give my love
To Inez and your mother and my friends.
Bartolo also sends his greetings to you.
I would have written better and more simple
Except my head spins like a dancing top
And my hand trembles ... I am oh, so weak ...

Alun Lewis

For Johnny

*John Pudney scribbled this poem on the back of an envelope during
an air-raid on London in 1941. He has said of it: 'There never was
a particular Johnny: it was meant for them all.'*

Do not despair
For Johnny-head-in-air;
He sleeps as sound
As Johnny underground.

Fetch out no shroud
For Johnny-in-the-cloud;
And keep your tears
For him in after years.

Better by far
For Johnny-the-bright-star,
To keep your head,
And see his children fed.

John Pudney

Security

Before flying over enemy-held territory, aircrews left behind all personal belongings which, in the event of capture, might give information to the enemy. As an Intelligence Officer in the R.A.F., John Pudney would be responsible for ensuring that this was done.

Empty your pockets, Tom, Dick and Harry,
Strip your identity; leave it behind.
Lawyer, garage-hand, grocer, don't tarry
With your own country, your own kind.

Leave all your letters. Suburb and township,
Green fen and grocery, slipway and bay,
Hot spring and prairie, smoke stack and coal tip,
Leave in our keeping while you're away

Tom, Dick and Harry, plain names and numbers,
Pilot, observer, and gunner depart.
Their personal litter only encumbers
Somebody's head, somebody's heart.

John Pudney

Missing

This poem was written at a time when heavy attacks were being made on the German battleship Scharnhorst *and losses among aircrews were severe.*

Less said the better.
The bill unpaid, the dead letter,
No roses at the end
Of Smith, my friend.

Last words don't matter,
And there are none to flatter.
Words will not fill the post
Of Smith, the ghost.

For Smith, our brother,
Only son of loving mother,
The ocean lifted, stirred,
Leaving no word.

John Pudney

Love of Country — One

I saw it after they had carried the hay,
The old blind wains behind a tractor doddering, creaking,
I saw the thunder come and hasten the end of the day,
The last of an era. I heard men speaking

No longer of fly or root, of seed or pest,
But of how much the live and dead stock fetched at the sale,
And there was no more heartbreak in their zest
Than zest in their ale.

I saw the fields that would never crop again,
The haywains split for firewood and the tractor rusting.
I saw the new masters swarming in gumboots in the rain
Indifferently plotting the new era, trusting
To blueprints stained by tea spills and the assent
Of sub-committees whose tobacco-tainted breath
By Eazle Wood and by Coldharbour went,
Regularizing death.

Would it ever be the same again, the same
Farmsteads and cottages sending their men to Agincourt:
Men who at the ends of the earth recalled the name
Of Coldharbour or Eazle Wood, who bought
Strange shiny trifles for red-faced girls who ran
To early milkings, and at harvest rode the loaded wains?
Love all lost in the development plan.
Of the lovers' lanes?

John Pudney

Love of Country — Two

Five feet down are the roots of concrete
Of Eazlewood Crescent, Coldharbour Way,
Plaza Parade, the shops on the corner
All go five feet into clay.

Five feet down are the roots they fought for,
And men died dreaming of Plaza Parade.
Womenfolk clung to bombed Eazlewood Crescent
Through raid after bombing raid.

John Pudney

Aunts Watching Television

The aunts who knew not Africa
But spoke of having been to Weymouth in the spring —
Not last spring but the year the lilac was so good —
Who never saw prize-fighters in a ring,
But could recall a fox-hunt in the neighbourhood.

Two aunts who never went abroad,
Nor travelled far in love, nor were much wronged, nor sinned
A lot — but for such peccadillos as to damn,
With tiny oaths, late frost or some chill wind,
Slugs at the dahlias or wasps at homemade jam.

Two aunts who, after silences,
Spoke knowingly of angels passing overhead:
But who prayed little and slept well, were worried less
By death than weeds: but hoped to die in bed,
Untouched by magic or economic stress.

This age's beneficiaries
For whom our century endows this box of dreams,
Conferring prize-fighters, dancers of unimaginable grace,
Glimpses of Africa, of football teams,
Of statesmen, of the finish of a classic race.

Vestals of the impalpable,
Dazed by its prodigality, by acrobats
On bicycles, by lovers speaking Shakespeare's lines,
Mazed by murders, by speeches from democrats ,
Wooed by cooking hints and the Paris dress designs.

Flirt on, soft spinsters, flirt with time.
Order the crowded hours, vicariously tranced.
Know Africa and judge which prize-fighter was hurt,
How well the latest ballerina danced,
How cake, or love, was made. O flirt, my two aunts, flirt!

John Pudney

Stormy Day

O look how the loops and balloons of bloom
Bobbing on long strings from the finger-ends
And knuckles of the lurching cherry-tree
Heap and hug, elbow and part, this wild day,
Like a careless carillon cavorting;
And the beaded whips of the beeches splay
And dip like anchored weed round a drowned rock,
And hovering effortlessly the rooks
Hang on the wind's effrontery as if
On hooks, then loose their hold and slide away
Like sleet sidewards down the warm swimming sweep
Of wind. O it is a lovely time when
Out of the sunk and rigid sumps of thought
Our hearts rise and race with new sounds and sights
And signs, tingling delightedly at the sting
And crunch of springless carts on gritty roads,
The caught kite dangling in the skinny wires,
The swipe of a swallow across the eyes,

Striped awnings stretched on lawns. New things surprise
And stop us everywhere. In the parks
The fountains scoop and flower like rockets
Over the oval ponds whose even skin
Is pocked and goosefleshed by their niggling rain
That frocks a naked core of statuary.
And at jetty's jut, roped and ripe for hire,
The yellow boats lie yielding and lolling,
Jilted and jolted like jellies. But look!
There! Do you see, crucified on palings,
Motionless news-posters announcing
That now the frozen armies melt and meet
And smash? Go home now, for, try as you may,
You will not shake off that fact to-day.
Behind you limps that dog with tarry paw,
As behind him, perfectly-timed, follows
The dumb shadow that mimes him all the way.

W. R. Rodgers

Prisoners of War

*John Jarmain was killed in Normandy shortly after the Allied
landings on June 6th, 1944.*

Like shabby ghosts down dried-up river beds
The tired procession slowly leaves the field;
Dazed and abandoned, just a count of heads,
They file away, these who have done their last,
To that grey safety where the days are sealed,
Where no word enters, and the urgent past
Is relieved day by day against the clock
Whose hours are meaningless, whose measured race
Brings nearer nothing, only serves to mock.

It is ended now. There's no more need to choose,
To fend and think and act: no need to hate.
Now all their will is worthless, none will lose
And none will suffer though their courage fail.
The tension in the brain is loosened now,
Its taut decisions slack: no more alone
— How I and each of us has been alone
Like lone trees which the lightnings all assail —
They are herded now and have no more to give.
Even fear is past. And death, so long so near,
Has suddenly receded to its station
In the misty end of life. For these will live,
They are quit of killing and sudden mutilation;
They no longer cower at the sound of a shell in the air,
They are safe. And in the glimmer at time's end
They will return — old, worn maybe, but sure —
And gather their bits of broken lives to mend.

Sicily. August–October 1943. John Jarmain

El Alamein

The battle of El Alamein, in which Jarmain fought, inflicted the first decisive defeat on the German and Italian armies. So great was the rejoicing in England that the church bells were specially rung in celebration.

There are flowers now, they say, at Alamein;
Yes, flowers in the minefields now.
So those that come to view that vacant scene,
Where death remains and agony has been
Will find the lilies grow —
Flowers, and nothing that we know.

So they rang the bells for us and Alamein,
Bells which we could not hear:
And to those that heard the bells what could it mean,
That name of loss and pride, El Alamein?
— Not the murk and harm of war,
But their hope, their own warm prayer.

It will become a staid historic name,
That crazy sea of sand!
Like Troy or Agincourt its single fame
Will be the garland for our brow, our claim,
On us a fleck of glory to the end:
And there our dead will keep their holy ground.

But this is not the place that we recall,
The crowded desert crossed with foaming tracks,
The one blotched building, lacking half a wall,
The grey-faced men, sand powdered over all;
The tanks, the guns, the trucks,
The black, dark-smoking wrecks.

So be it: none but us has known that land:
El Alamein will still be only ours
And those ten days of chaos in the sand.
Others will come who cannot understand,
Will halt beside the rusty minefield wires
And find there — flowers.

Mareth, Tunisia. March 1943. John Jarmain

The Airman

I do not know — would that I knew! —
To what end I have learnt this skill,
Or why I climb each day into the sky
To find one who shall kill me, or to kill.
If only we might think it true
That it's a simple thing to die
In a good cause — both he and I!
But that's not so. Too well we know
It's the old game that was first played by Cain,
By Greek and Trojan, English, French and Scot,
Again and yet again,
And all — for any good the world has got —
Except for the game's sake, always in vain.
Then to no end, for no cause, without hate
We two shall meet among the clouds, and fall,
Since to our death, one or both, fall we must.
And yet, can that be all?
Out of the dust of him who dies
This time let no avenger rise;
But somehow, some day, soon or late
Since all things change and wax and wane,
And happiness is the child of pain,
May it not be that those born after,
Because we lived and fought and died
Led by hope, not by hate or pride,
Shall grow wise and return to laughter?

R. C. Trevelyan

The Horns of Lud

Lud was a mythical king of Britain long before the Romans came and is said to have given his name to the chief town, Lud's Town becoming London. His name is also commemorated in Ludgate (Lud's Gate) near which his body was allegedly buried.

I

Air-raid

London; Lud's Dun: the hoar and heavy drum vowels roll
Alarms from Roman, Saxon, Norman. Kings have come
And down upon this town of mist and marsh found home —
Yielding to old, uncouth and Celtic Sea-God's call.

And now red London burns, and red from her red flood
Her guns are sacrificial horns. Lud's trumpets blare
And boom; her banner searchlights thrust and thresh and flare;
Her smoke, a huge black boom, unfurls its sombre hood.

With siren songs the morning wells up worn and slow
With all the scurrying bombers fled in insect drone:
London's black rose, still stalked, yet sways against green dawn
And Thames drains grief from each its banks in seaward flow.

Yet London, dark and vast, Lud's town, now brim with tears,
Through bomb-smoke pall will burst, and shimmer through
    New Years.

Francis Berry

85

War

Going about our business day by day
We think, deluded heart, that we forget
The peril that besets us — and beset
Our fathers once, when they too turned away
To watch our childish games and dreamt that all
Our innocence could prevent the heaven's fall.

But heaven fell. Virtue and wealth and power
All fell; and we, too young to understand
Such waste of heritage, ran out to stand
Proud in our fathers' presence in their hour
Of victory — for some had called it so:
Victory or defeat, we were too young to know.

Only we knew a strangeness in their arms
And on their lips a tang of bitter words,
As though in putting up their weary swords
They found not peace, but greater strife that harms
With deeper wounds, being more deeply bred.
Escaping death they came home to the dead.

Thereafter in the shadow of their guilt
We grew, a lonely generation born
Out of violence, into violence thrown,
Till all the sacrificial blood they spilt
To save our blood seemed only shed in vain.
The murderous ritual had begun again.

To-day I go about the busy street
And know whoever walks beside me there
Walks in a treadmill of returning fear

86

Wherein once more the generations meet
And cry: 'O Man! from tyrannous war release
Our troubled hearts and grant our children peace!'

J. C. Hall

The Son

I found the letter in a cardboard box,
Unfamous history. I read the words.
The ink was frail and brown, the paper dry
After so many years of being kept.
The letter was a soldier's, from the Front —
Conveyed his love, and disappointed hope
Of getting leave. *It's cancelled now*, he wrote
My luck is at the bottom of the sea.

Outside the sun was hot; the world looked bright;
I heard a radio, and someone laughed.
I did not sing, or laugh, or love the sun.
Within the quiet room I thought of him,
My father killed, and all the other men
Whose luck was at the bottom of the sea.

Clifford Dyment

The Swans

Midstream they met. Challenger and Champion,
They fought a war for honour
Fierce, sharp, but with no honour:
Each had a simple aim and sought it quickly.
The combat over the victor sailed away
Broken, but placid as is the gift of swans,
Leaving his rival to his shame alone.

I listened for a song, according to story,
But this swan's death was out of character —
No giving up the grace of life
In a sad lingering music.
I saw the beaten swan rise on the water
As though to outreach pain, its webbed feet
Banging the river helplessly, its wings
Loose in a last hysteria. Then the neck
Was floating like a rope and the swan was dead.
It drifted away and all around it swan's down
Bobbed on the river like children's boats.

Clifford Dyment

The Monuments of Hiroshima

*The atomic age began on August 6th, 1945, when at least 60,000
men, women and children were killed by the atomic bomb which
was exploded over the Japanese seaport of Hiroshima: 100,000 more,
many of whom have since died, were injured.*

The roughly estimated ones, who do not sort well with our
    common phrases,
Who are by no means eating roots of dandelion, or pushing up
    the daisies.

The more or less anonymous, to whom no human idiom can
    apply,
Who neither passed away, or on,
    nor went before, nor vanished on a sigh.

Little of peace for them to rest in, less of them to rest in peace:
Dust to dust a swift transition, ashes to ash with awful ease.

Their only monument will be of others' casting —
A Tower of Peace, a Hall of Peace, a Bridge of Peace
   — who might have wished for something lasting,
Like a wooden box.

D. J. Enright

Stanley Matthews

Association football is played in most but not all the countries in the world. For the benefit of readers in countries where the game is not particularly popular it should be explained that Stanley Matthews is one of the game's greatest artists. The poem truthfully describes the extraordinary fascination Matthews induces in his opponents.

Alan Ross is a sports writer for a well-known Sunday newspaper and writes poetry in his spare time. In this poem he seems to be combining business and pleasure.

Not often *con brio*, but *andante, andante*, horseless, though jockey-
    like and jaunty,
Straddling the touchline, live margin not out of the game, nor
    quite in,
Made by him green and magnetic, stroller
Indifferent as a cat dissembling, rolling
A little as on deck, till the mouse, the ball, slides palely to him
And shyly almost, with deprecatory cough, he is off.

Head of a Perugino,[1] with faint flair
Of the nostrils, as though Lipizzaner-like[2]
    he sniffed at the air,
Finding it good beneath him, he draws

---

[1] An Italian Renaissance painter.
[2] Lippizzaners are the magnificent horses used in the Spanish Court Riding School, Vienna.

Defenders towards him, the ball a bait
They refuse like a poisoned chocolate, retreating, till he slows his
    gait
To a walk, inviting the tackle, inciting it.

Till, unrefusable, dangling the ball at the instep,
He is charged — and stiffening so slowly
It is barely perceptible, he executes with a squirm
Of the hips, a twist more suggestive than apparent, that lazily
    disdainful move *toreros*[1] term
    a Veronica — it's enough.
Only emptiness following him, pursuing some scent
Of his own, he weaves in towards, not away from, fresh tacklers,
Who, turning about to gain time, are by him harried, pursued
    not pursuers.

Now gathers speed, nursing the ball as he cruises,
Eyes judging distance, noting the gaps, the spaces
Vital for colleagues to move to, slowing a trace,
As from Vivaldi[2] to Dibdin,[3] pausing,
    and leisurely, leisurely, swings
To the left upright his centre, on hips
His hands, observing the goalkeeper spring,
    heads rising vainly to the ball's curve
Just as it's plucked from them; and dispassionately
Back to his mark he trots, whistling through closed lips.

Trim as a yacht, with similar lightness
    — of keel, of reaction to surface — with salt air
Tanned, this incomparable player, in decline fair
    to look at, nor in decline either,

[1] Bullfighters.
[2] A famous Italian violinist and composer.
[3] A well-known writer of popular songs, especially sea shanties.

Improving like wine with age, has come far —
    born to one, a barber, who boxed,
Not with such filial magnificence, but well.
'The greatest of all time', *meraviglioso* Matthews —
    Stoke City,[1] Blackpool[1] and England.
Expressionless enchanter, weaving as on strings
Conceptual patterns to a private music, heard
Only by him, to whose slowly emerging theme
He rehearses steps, soloist in compulsions of a dream.

                           Alan Ross

Slow Train to Portsmouth

Alan Ross was in the Royal Navy during the war. He served in destroyers and was engaged in the Battle of the Barents Sea while escorting a Russia-bound convoy.

    The sky rinsed as a blue-jean collar,
    And the train, on this April Monday, idling,
    With nothing better to do than to follow
    The curves and windings of sidling
    Rivers, and, sniffing marsh air, at snail's
    Pace clank through the flapping
    Washing, proud as *Potemkin*[2] —

    Swans glide in flotillas on lapping
    Waters, and the estuaries hang up their sails,
    Indigo, rust and cerulean,
    And clouds, like transfers, soak
    On surfaces of inlets where beached boats
    Vamp the sun on a morning that floats.

[1] The league clubs for which Matthews has played.
[2] A Russian battleship of the Czarist navy whose mutinous ratings are now regarded in the U.S.S.R. as national heroes.

Hamble Halt, Bursledon, Bitterne —
We edge through rushes, inhaling the paint
From upturned houseboats, ketches, yawls,
And hear soon the first faint
Siren notes from Pompey harbour — the train crawls
Past old Landing Craft, their flaking keels
No longer chipped after raking patrols,
But flopped on the mud like veteran seals,

And I am suddenly returned there,
To a crumbling shore and a barracks where
— Was it in the same lifetime? —
We dawdled between ships, without rhyme
Or reason filling in each day,
Awaiting the signal that would sever
The links, and whisk us from the bay
For an unknown time that might be for ever.

Once more I am prey
To this dockyard smell, so that I crick
My neck to lean from the train,
And feast my eyes on the derricks
That line the quays among bollards and cranes,
And catch a glimpse, as they ride at anchor,
Of two destroyers, a frigate and tanker,
My eyes lingering on them (as should they meet
Old lovers, not often remembered).
This morning of rusting dismembered
Vessels, languishing here from an ailing fleet,
Takes on fresh tenderness for me —
Longing for faces I shall not again see.

Alan Ross

On a Friend's Escape from Drowning off the Norfolk Coast

Came up that cold sea at Cromer like a running grave
    Beside him as he struck
Wildly towards the shore, but the blackcapped wave
    Crossed him and swung him back,
And he saw his son digging in the castled dirt that could save.
    Then the farewell rock
Rose a last time to his eyes. As he cried out
    A pawing gag of the sea
Smothered his cry and he sank in his own shout
    Like a dying airman. Then she
Deep near her son asleep on the hourglass sand
    Was wakened by whom
Save the Fate who knew that this was the wrong time:
    And opened her eyes
On the death of her son's begetter. Up she flies
    Into the hydra-headed
Grave as he closes his life upon her who for
    Life has so richly bedded him.
But she drove through his drowning like Orpheus and tore
    Back by the hair
Her escaping bridegroom. And on the sand their son
    Stood laughing where
He was almost an orphan. Then the three lay down
    On that cold sand,
Each holding the other by a living hand.

George Barker

Born Yesterday

(For Sally Amis)

Tightly-folded bud,
I have wished you something
None of the others would:
Not the usual stuff
About being beautiful
Or running off a spring
Of innocence or love —
They will all wish you that,
And should it prove possible,
Well, you're a lucky girl.

But if it shouldn't, then
May you be ordinary;
Have like other women
An average of talents:
Not ugly, not good-looking,
Nothing uncustomary
To pull you off your balance,
That, unworkable itself,
Stops all the rest from working.
In fact, may you be dull —
If that is what a skilled,
Vigilant, flexible,
Unemphasized, enthralled
Catching of happiness is called.

Philip Larkin

Toads

The desire to escape from what seems to be a strangling routine of respectability is common enough in poets — W. H. Davies for example — but is rarely expressed with the vehemence Philip Larkin uses here. This view of life may not be particularly admirable but each poet is entitled to state his own views in his own way. The reader is not obliged to follow the poem but only to respond to the poem's challenge.

Why should I let the toad *work*
   Squat on my life?
Can't I use my wit as a pitchfork
   And drive the brute off?

Six days of the week it soils
   With its sickening poison —
Just for paying a few bills!
   That's out of proportion.

Lots of folk live on their wits:
   Lecturers, lispers,
Losels, loblolly-men, louts —
   They don't end as paupers.

Lots of folk live up lanes
   With a fire in a bucket;
Eat windfalls and tinned sardines
   They seem to like it.

Their nippers have got bare feet,
   Their unspeakable wives
Are skinny as whippets — and yet
   No one actually *starves*.

Ah, were I courageous enough
   To shout *Stuff your pension*!
But I know, all too well, that's the stuff
   That dreams are made on:

For something sufficiently toad-like
   Squats in me too;
Its hunkers are heavy as hard luck,
   And cold as snow,

And will never allow me to blarney
   My way to getting
The fame and the girl and the money
   All at one sitting.

I don't say, one bodies the other
   One's spiritual truth;
But I do say it's hard to lose either,
   When you have both.

Philip Larkin

At Grass

The eye can hardly pick them out
From the cold shade they shelter in,
Till wind distresses tail and mane;
Then one crops grass, and moves about
— The other seeming to look on —
And stands anonymous again.

Yet fifteen years ago, perhaps
Two dozen distances sufficed
To fable them: faint afternoons
Of Cups and Stakes and Handicaps,
Whereby their names were artificed
To inlay faded, classic Junes —

Silks at the start: against the sky
Numbers and parasols: outside,
Squadrons of empty cars, and heat,
And littered grass: then the long cry
Hanging unhushed till it subside
To stop-press columns on the street.

Do memories plague their ears like flies?
They shake their heads. Dusk brims the shadows.
Summer by summer all stole away,
The starting-gates, the crowds and cries —
All but the unmolesting meadows.
Almanacked, their names live; they

Have slipped their names, and stand at ease,
Or gallop for what must be joy,
And not a field-glass sees them home,
Or curious stop-watch prophesies:
Only the groom, and the groom's boy,
With bridles in the evening come.

Philip Larkin

Wires

The widest prairies have electric fences,
For though old cattle know they must not stray,
Young steers are always scenting purer water
Not here but anywhere. Beyond the wires

Leads them to blunder up against the wires
Whose muscle-shredding violence gives no quarter.
Young steers become old cattle from that day,
Electric limits to their widest senses.

Philip Larkin

This above all is precious and remarkable

This above all is precious and remarkable,
How we put ourselves in one another's care,
How in spite of everything we trust each other.

Fishermen at whatever point they are dipping and lifting
On the dark green swell they partly think of as home
Hear the gale warnings that fly to them like gulls.

The scientists study the weather for love of studying it,
And not specially for love of the fishermen,
And the wireless engineers do the transmission for love of
wireless,

But how it adds up is that when the terrible white malice
Of the waves high as cliffs is let loose to seek a victim,
The fishermen are somewhere else and so not drowned.

98

And why should this chain of miracles be easier to believe
Than that my darling should come to me as naturally
As she trusts a restaurant not to poison her?

They are simply examples of well-known types of miracle,
The two of them,
That can happen at any time of the day or night.

John Wain

Emperors of the Island

A political parable to be read aloud

> There is the story of a deserted island
> where five men walked down to the bay.
>
> The story of this island is
> that three men would two men slay.
>
> Three men dug two graves in the sand,
> three men stood on the sea wet rock,
> three shadows moved away.
>
> There is the story of a deserted island
> where three men walked down to the bay.
>
> The story of this island is
> that two men would one man slay.
>
> Two men dug one grave in the sand.
> two men stood on the sea wet rock,
> two shadows moved away.

There is the story of a deserted island
where two men walked down to the bay.

The story of this island is
that one man would one man slay.

One man dug one grave in the sand,
one man stood on the sea wet rock,
one shadow moved away.

There is the story of a deserted island
where four ghosts walked down to the bay.

The story of this island is
that four ghosts would one man slay.

Four ghosts dug one grave in the sand,
four ghosts stood on the sea wet rock;
five ghosts moved away.

Dannie Abse

Wreath Makers: Leeds Market

A cocksure boy in the gloom of the gilded market bends
With blunt fingers a bow of death, and the flowers work with
  him.
They fashion a grave of grass with dead bracken and fine ferns.

An old woman with a mouthful of wires and a clutch of irises
Mourns in perpetual black, and her fists with the sunken rings
Rummage in the fragrant workbasket of a wreath.

A laughing Flora dangles a cross between her thighs
Like a heavy child, feeds it with pale plump lilies, crimson
Roses, wraps it in greenery and whips it with wires.

And here a grieving flower god with a lyre in his arms
Fumbles mute strings in the rough-gentle machine of his fingers,
His eyes wet violets, and in his mouth a last carnation ...

Mourners all, they know not why they mourn,
But work and breathe the perfumes of their trade
(Those flower-vines, through which death more keenly speaks)

With suitable dispassion; though they know their emblems fade,
And they at last must bear a yellowed wreath
That other hands, and other harvesters have made.

James Kirkup

African Beggar

Sprawled in the dust outside the Syrian store,
a target for small children, dogs and flies,
a heap of verminous rags and matted hair,
he watches us with cunning, reptile eyes,
his noseless, smallpoxed face creased in a sneer.

Sometimes he shows his yellow stumps of teeth
and whines for alms, perceiving that we bear
the curse of pity; a grotesque mask of death,
with hands like claws about his begging-bowl.

But often he is lying all alone
within the shadow of a crumbling wall,

lost in the trackless jungle of his pain,
clutching the pitiless red earth in vain
and whimpering like a stricken animal.

Raymond Tong

An Old Man's Hands

His hands are those of my father's generation
And speak to me in pity. Seventy summers
Have laid a skin of brown on them, the knuckles
Are bare and smooth with life, pared like old wood
And sanded down to silk and ash. One finger
Is gripped by an outmoded ring, wide, serviceable
Gold. Work has ebbed from those fingers, as the sea
Down ribs and groins of sand. Life recedes from them.
What can they do now but lift in the spires of prayer
Passive to the touch of love? Innocent hands
Like shells, two lobes, which joined, nourish the pearl,
The core of light, eternity's quiet seed.
And over the skin, the mark of suffering man
Burns in a livid scar. Close, louring, knitted,
Clenched in the face of the world, they hold back all
Like gnarled and watchful dogs, knotted on the knees,
Guarding the secrets of the inviolate self,
Until, unsealed in sleep, unfolding like flowers,
And opening in the last frank gesture of man,
They give back all, yield all at last, surrendering
The knotted self to eternity, unbound
In death's calm, final generosity.

Margaret Stanley-Wrench

The Death of the Hired Man

A hired man is a worker employed on farms in the United States who, since he has no home of his own, receives board and lodging from his employer in addition to wages. Having few ties he frequently moves from farm to farm, working his way across the American Continent. Although he has the advantage of variety, it is a rootless and lonely existence compared with that of an English farm-worker with his cottage and family.

Robert Frost was himself a farmer in Vermont, U.S.A.

Mary sat musing on the lamp-flame at the table
Waiting for Warren. When she heard his step,
She ran on tip-toe down the darkened passage
To meet him in the doorway with the news
And put him on his guard. 'Silas is back.'
She pushed him outward with her through the door
And shut it after her. 'Be kind,' she said.
She took the market things from Warren's arms
And set them on the porch, then drew him down
To sit beside her on the wooden steps.

'When was I ever anything but kind to him?
But I'll not have the fellow back,' he said.
'I told him so last haying, didn't I?
"If he left then," I said, "that ended it."
What good is he? Who else will harbour him
At his age for the little he can do?
What help he is there's no depending on.
Off he goes always when I need him most.
"He thinks he ought to earn a little pay,
Enough at least to buy tobacco with,

So he won't have to beg and be beholden."
"All right," I say, "I can't afford to pay
Any fixed wages, though I wish I could."
"Someone else can." "Then someone else will have to."
I shouldn't mind his bettering himself
If that was what it was. You can be certain,
When he begins like that, there's someone at him
Trying to coax him off with pocket-money, —
In haying time, when any help is scarce.
In winter he comes back to us. I'm done.'
'Sh! not so loud: he'll hear you,' Mary said.

'I want him to: he'll have to soon or late.'

'He's worn out. He's asleep beside the stove.
When I came up from Rowe's I found him here,
Huddled against the barn-door fast asleep,
A miserable sight, and frightening, too —
You needn't smile — I didn't recognize him —
I wasn't looking for him — and he's changed.
Wait till you see.'

                              'Where did you say he'd been?'

'He didn't say. I dragged him to the house,
And gave him tea and tried to make him smoke.
I tried to make him talk about his travels. ·
Nothing would do: he just kept nodding off.'

'What did he say? Did he say anything?'

'But little.'

'Anything? Mary, confess
He said he'd come to ditch the meadow for me.'

'Warren!'
'But did he? I just want to know.'

'Of course he did. What would you have him say?
Surely you wouldn't grudge the poor old man
Some humble way to save his self-respect.
He added, if you really care to know,
He meant to clear the upper pasture, too.
That sounds like something you have heard before?
Warren, I wish you could have heard the way
He jumbled everything. I stopped to look
Two or three times — he made me feel so queer —
To see if he was talking in his sleep.
He ran on Harold Wilson — you remember —
The boy you had in haying four years since.
He's finished school, and teaching in his college.
Silas declares you'll have to get him back.
He says they two will make a team for work:
Between them they will lay this farm as smooth!
The way he mixed that in with other things.
He thinks young Wilson a likely lad, though daft
On education — you know how they fought
All through July under the blazing sun,
Silas up on the cart to build the load,
Harold along beside to pitch it on.'

'Yes, I took care to keep well out of earshot.'

'Well, those days trouble Silas like a dream.
You wouldn't think they would. How some things linger!

Harold's young college boy's assurance piqued him.
After so many years he still keeps finding
Good arguments he sees he might have used.
I sympathize. I know just how it feels
To think of the right thing to say too late.
Harold's associated in his mind with Latin.
He asked me what I thought of Harold's saying
He studied Latin like the violin
Because he liked it — that an argument!
He said he couldn't make the boy believe
He could find water with a hazel prong —
Which showed how much good school had ever done him.
He wanted to go over that. But most of all
He thinks if he could have another chance
To teach him how to build a load of hay — '

'I know, that's Silas' one accomplishment.
He bundles every forkful in its place,
And tags and numbers it for future reference,
So he can find and easily dislodge it
In the unloading. Silas does that well.
He takes it out in bunches like big birds' nests.
You never see him standing on the hay
He's trying to lift, straining to lift himself.'

'He thinks if he could teach him that, he'd be
Some good perhaps to someone in the world.
He hates to see a boy the fool of books.
Poor Silas, so concerned for other folk,
And nothing to look backward to with pride,
And nothing to look forward to with hope,
So now and never any different.'

Part of a moon was falling down the west,
Dragging the whole sky with it to the hills.
Its light poured softly in her lap. She saw it
And spread her apron to it. She put out her hand
Among the harp-like morning-glory strings,
Taut with the dew from garden bed to eaves,
As if she played unheard some tenderness
That wrought on him beside her in the night.
'Warren,' she said, 'he has come home to die:
You needn't be afraid he'll leave you this time.'

'Home,' he mocked gently.

       'Yes, what else but home?
It all depends on what you mean by home.
Of course he's nothing to us, any more
Than was the hound that came a stranger to us
Out of the woods, worn out upon the trail.'

 'Home is the place where, when you have to go there,
 They have to take you in.'

        'I should have called it
Something you somehow haven't to deserve.'

Warren leaned out and took a step or two,
Picked up a little stick, and brought it back
And broke it in his hand and tossed it by.
'Silas has better claim on us you think
Than on his brother? Thirteen little miles
As the road winds would bring him to his door.
Silas has walked that far no doubt to-day.
Why didn't he go there? His brother's rich,
A somebody — director in the bank.'

'He never told us that.'

'We know it though.'

'I think his brother ought to help, of course.
I'll see to that if there is need. He ought of right
To take him in, and might be willing to —
He may be better than appearances.
But have some pity on Silas. Do you think
If he had any pride in claiming kin
Or anything he looked for from his brother,
He'd keep so still about him all this time?'

'I wonder what's between them.'

'I can tell you.
Silas is what he is — we wouldn't mind him —
But just the kind that kinsfolk can't abide.
He never did a thing so very bad.
He don't know why he isn't quite as good
As anybody. Worthless though he is,
He won't be made ashamed to please his brother.'

'I can't think Si ever hurt anyone.'

'No, but he hurt my heart the way he lay
And rolled his old head on that sharp-edged chair-back.
He wouldn't let me put him on the lounge.
You must go in and see what you can do.
I made the bed up for him there to-night.
You'll be surprised at him — how much he's broken.
His working days are done; I'm sure of it.'

'I'd not be in a hurry to say that.'

'I haven't been. Go, look, see for yourself.
But, Warren, please remember how it is:

He's come to help you ditch the meadow.
He has a plan. You mustn't laugh at him.
He may not speak of it, and then he may.
I'll sit and see if that small sailing cloud
Will hit or miss the moon.'

It hit the moon.
Then there were three there, making a dim row,
The moon, the little silver cloud, and she.

Warren returned — too soon, it seemed to her,
Slipped to her side, caught up her hand and waited.

'Warren?' she questioned.

'Dead,' was all he answered.

Robert Frost

Two Tramps in Mud Time

Out of the mud two strangers came
And caught me splitting wood in the yard.
And one of them put me off my aim
By hailing cheerily 'Hit them hard!'
I knew pretty well why he dropped behind
And let the other go on a way.
I knew pretty well what he had in mind:
He wanted to take my job for pay.

Good blocks of beech it was I split,
As large around as the chopping block;
And every piece I squarely hit
Fell splinterless as a cloven rock.

The blows that a life of self-control
Spares to strike for the common good
That day, giving a loose to my soul,
I spent on the unimportant wood.

The sun was warm but the wind was chill.
You know how it is with an April day
When the sun is out and the wind is still,
You're one month on in the middle of May.
But if you so much as dare to speak,
A cloud comes over the sunlit arch.
A wind comes off a frozen peak,
And you're two months back in the middle of March.

A bluebird comes tenderly up to alight
And fronts the wind to unruffle a plume
His song so pitched as not to excite
A single flower as yet to bloom.
It is snowing a flake: and he half knew
Winter was only playing possum.
Except in color he isn't blue,
But he wouldn't advise a thing to blossom.

The water for which we may have to look
In summertime with a witching-wand,
In every wheelrut's now a brook,
In every print of a hoof a pond.
Be glad of water, but don't forget
The lurking frost in the earth beneath
That will steal forth after the sun is set
And show on the water its crystal teeth.

The time when most I loved my task
These two must make me love it more
By coming with what they came to ask.
You'd think I never had felt before
The weight of an ax-head poised aloft,
The grip on earth of outspread feet.
The life of muscles rocking soft
And smooth and moist in vernal heat.

Out of the woods two hulking tramps
(From sleeping God knows where last night,
But not long since in the lumber camps).
They thought all chopping was theirs of right.
Men of the woods and lumberjacks,
They judged me by their appropriate tool.
Except as a fellow handled an ax,
They had no way of knowing a fool.

Nothing on either side was said.
They knew they had but to stay their stay
And all their logic would fill my head:
As that I had no right to play
With what was another man's work for gain.
My right might be love but theirs was need.
And where the two exist in twain
Theirs was the better right — agreed.

But yield who will to their separation,
My object in living is to unite
My avocation and my vocation
As my two eyes make one in sight.

Only where love and need are one,
And the work is play for mortal stakes,
Is the deed ever really done
For Heaven and the future's sakes.

Robert Frost

'Out, Out —'

The buzz-saw snarled and rattled in the yard
And made dust and dropped stove-length sticks of wood,
Sweet-scented stuff when the breeze drew across it.
And from there those that lifted eyes could count
Five mountain ranges one behind the other
Under the sunset far into Vermont.
And the saw snarled and rattled, snarled and rattled,
As it ran light, or had to bear a load.
And nothing happened: day was all but done.
Call it a day, I wish they might have said
To please the boy by giving him the half hour
That a boy counts so much when saved from work.
His sister stood beside them in her apron
To tell them 'Supper.' At the word, the saw,
As if to prove saws knew what supper meant,
Leaped out at the boy's hand, or seemed to leap —
He must have given the hand. However it was,
Neither refused the meeting. But the hand!
The boy's first outcry was a rueful laugh,
As he swung toward them holding up the hand
Half in appeal, but half as if to keep
The life from spilling. Then the boy saw all —
Since he was old enough to know, big boy
Doing a man's work, though a child at heart —

He saw all spoiled. 'Don't let him cut my hand off —
The doctor, when he comes. Don't let him, sister!'
So. But the hand was gone already.
The doctor put him in the dark of ether.
He lay and puffed his lips out with his breath.
And then — the watcher at his pulse took fright.
No one believed. They listened at his heart.
Little — less — nothing! — and that ended it.
No more to build on there. And they, since they
Were not the one dead, turned to their affairs.

Robert Frost

A Considerable Speck

(Microscopic)

A speck that would have been beneath my sight
On any but a paper sheet so white
Set off across what I had written there.
And I had idly poised my pen in air
To stop it with a period of ink
When something strange about it made me think.
This was no dust speck by my breathing blown,
But unmistakably a living mite
With inclinations it could call its own.
It paused as with suspicion of my pen,
And then came racing wildly on again
To where my manuscript was not yet dry;
Then paused again and either drank or smelt —
With loathing, for again it turned to fly.
Plainly with an intelligence I dealt.
It seemed too tiny to have room for feet,
Yet must have had a set of them complete
To express how much it didn't want to die.

It ran with terror and with cunning crept.
It faltered: I could see it hesitate;
Then in the middle of the open sheet
Cower down in desperation to accept
Whatever I accorded it of fate.
I have none of the tenderer-than-thou
Collectivistic regimenting love
With which the modern world is being swept.
But this poor microscopic item now!
Since it was nothing I knew evil of
I let it lie there till I hope it slept.
I have a mind myself and recognize
Mind when I meet with it in any guise.
No one can know how glad I am to find
On any sheet the least display of mind.

Robert Frost

The Exposed Nest

You were forever finding some new play,
So when I saw you down on hands and knees
In the meadow, busy with the new-cut hay,
Trying, I thought, to set it up on end,
I went to show you how to make it stay,
If that was your idea, against the breeze,
And, if you asked me, even help pretend
To make it root again and grow afresh.
But 'twas no make-believe with you to-day,
Nor was the grass itself your real concern,
Though I found your hand full of wilted fern,
Steel-bright June-grass, and blackening heads of clover.
'Twas a nest full of young birds on the ground

114

The cutter-bar had just gone champing over
(Miraculously without tasting flesh)
And left defenceless to the heat and light.
You wanted to restore them to their right
Of something interposed between their sight
And too much world at once — could means be found.
The way the nest-full every time we stirred
Stood up to us as to a mother-bird
Whose coming home has been too long deferred,
Made me ask would the mother-bird return
And care for them in such a change of scene
And might our meddling make her more afraid.
That was a thing we could not wait to learn.
We saw the risk we took in doing good,
But dared not spare to do the best we could
Though harm should come of it; so built the screen
You had begun, and gave them back their shade.
All this to prove we cared. Why is there then
No more to tell? We turned to other things.
I haven't any memory — have you? —
Of ever coming to the place again
To see if the birds lived the first night through,
And so at last to learn to use their wings.

Robert Frost

Chicago

Hog Butcher for the World,
Tool Maker, Stacker of Wheat,
Player with Railroads and the Nation's Freight Handler;
Stormy, husky, brawling,
City of the Big Shoulders:

They tell me you are wicked, and I believe them; for I have seen
your painted women under the gas lamps luring the farm boys.

And they tell me you are crooked, and I answer: Yes, it is true
I have seen the gunman kill and go free to kill again.

And they tell me you are brutal, and my reply is: On the faces of
women and children I have seen the marks of wanton hunger.

And having answered so I turn once more to those who sneer at
this my city, and I give them back the sneer and say to them:

Come and show me another city with lifted head singing so
proud to be alive and coarse and strong and cunning.

Flinging magnetic curses amid the toil of piling job on job, here
is a tall bold slugger set vivid against the little soft cities;

Fierce as a dog with tongue lapping for action, cunning as a
savage pitted against the wilderness,

Bareheaded,

Shovelling,

Wrecking,

Planning,

Building, breaking, rebuilding,

Under the smoke, dust all over his mouth, laughing with white
teeth,

Under the terrible burden of destiny laughing as a young man laughs,

Laughing even as an ignorant fighter laughs who has never lost
a battle,

Bragging and laughing that under his wrist is the pulse, and
under his ribs the heart of the people,

Laughing!

Laughing the stormy, husky, brawling laughter of Youth,
half-naked, sweating, proud to be Hog Butcher, Tool
Maker, Stacker of Wheat, Player with Railroads and Freight
Handler to the Nation.

Carl Sandburg

Four Preludes on Playthings
of the Wind

'The past is a bucket of ashes'

I

The woman named To-morrow
sits with a hairpin in her teeth
and takes her time
and does her hair the way she wants it
and fastens at last the last braid and coil
and puts the hairpin where it belongs
and turns and drawls: Well, what of it?
My grandmother, Yesterday, is gone.
What of it? Let the dead be dead.

II

The doors were cedar
and the panels strips of gold
and the girls were golden girls
and the panels read and the girls chanted:
    We are the greatest city,
    the greatest nation:
    nothing like us ever was.
The doors are twisted on broken hinges.
Sheets of rain swish through on the wind
    where the golden girls ran and the panels read:
    We are the greatest city,
    the greatest nation:
    nothing like us ever was.

III

It has happened before.
Strong men put up a city and got a nation together,

And paid singers to sing and women to warble:
 We are the greatest city,
 the greatest nation:
 nothing like us ever was.

And while the singers sang
and the strong men listened
and paid the singers well
and felt good about it all,
 there were rats and lizards who listened
 … and the only listeners left now
 … are … the rats … and the lizards.

And there are black crows
crying, 'Caw, caw',
bringing mud and sticks
building a nest
over the words carved
on the doors where the panels were cedar
and the strips on the panels were gold
and the golden girls came singing:
 We are the greatest city,
 the greatest nation:
 nothing like us ever was.

The only singers now are crows crying, 'Caw, caw',
And the sheets of rain whine in the wind and doorways.
And the only listeners now are … the rats … and the lizards.

IV

 The feet of the rats
 scribble on the door sills;
 the hieroglyphs of the rat footprints

chatter the pedigrees of the rats
and babble of the blood
and gabble of the breed
of the grandfathers and the great-grandfathers
of the rats

And the wind shifts
and the dust on a door sill shifts
and even the writing of the rat footprints
tells us nothing, nothing at all
about the greatest city, the greatest nation
where the strong men listened
and the women warbled: Nothing like us ever was.

Carl Sandburg

England Expects

Though Ogden Nash writes humorously the underlying purpose of his verse is serious enough. He finds humour a convenient disguise for the things he feels really strongly about.

Let us pause to consider the English,
Who when they pause to consider themselves they get all
reticently thrilled and tinglish,
Because every Englishman is convinced of one thing, viz.:
That to be an Englishman is to belong to the most exclusive club
there is:
A club to which benighted bounders of Frenchmen and Germans
and Italians et cetera cannot even aspire
to belong,
Because they don't even speak English, and the Americans are
worst of all because they speak it wrong.
Englishmen are distinguished by their traditions and ceremonials.

And also by their affection for their colonies and their contempt
for their colonials.

When foreigners ponder world affairs, why sometimes by doubts
they are smitten,

But Englishmen know instinctively that what the world needs
most is whatever is best for Great Britain.

They have a splendid navy and they conscientiously admire it,

And every English schoolboy knows that John Paul Jones[1] was
only an unfair American pirate.

English people disclaim sparkle and verve,

But speak without reservations of their Anglo-Saxon reserve.

After listening to little groups of English ladies and gentlemen
at cocktail parties and in hotels and Pullmans, of defining
Anglo-Saxon reserve I despair,

But I think it consists of assuming that nobody else is there,

And I shudder to think where Anglo-Saxon reserve ends when
I consider where it begins,

Which is in a few high-pitched statements of what one's income
is and just what foods give one a rash and whether one and
one's husband or wife sleep in a double bed or twins.

All good young Englishmen go to Oxford or Cambridge and
they all write and publish books before their graduation,

And I often wondered how they did it until I realized that they
have to do it because their genteel accents are so developed
that they can no longer understand each other's spoken
words so the written word is their only means of inter-
communication.

England is the last home of the aristocracy, and the art of pro-
tecting the aristocracy from the encroachments of commerce
has been raised to quite an art,

[1] A rather successful American naval officer who fought against Britain in the
American War of Independence.

Because in America a rich butter-and-egg man is only a rich
butter-and-egg man or at most an honorary LL.D. of some
hungry university, but in England why before he knows it
he is Sir Benjamin Buttery, Bart.
Anyhow, I think the English people are sweet,
And we might as well get used to them because when they slip
and fall they always land on their own or somebody else's feet.

Ogden Nash

Kindly unhitch that star, buddy

I hardly suppose I know anybody who wouldn't rather be a
success than a failure,
Just as I suppose every piece of crabgrass in the garden would
much rather be an azalea,
And in celestial circles all the run-of-the-mill angels would
rather be archangels or at least cherubim and seraphim,
And in the legal world all the little processs-servers hope to grow
up into great big bailiffim and sheriffim.
Indeed, everybody wants to be a wow,
But not everybody knows exactly how.
Some people think they will eventually wear diamonds instead
of rhinestones
Only by everlastingly keeping their noses to their grhinestones,
And other people think they will be able to put in more time at
Palm Beach and the Ritz
By not paying too much attention to attendance at the office but
rather in being brilliant by starts and fits.
Some people after a full day's work sit up all night getting a
college education by correspondence,
While others seem to think they'll get just as far by devoting
their evenings to the study of the difference in temperament
between brunettance and blondance.

Some stake their all on luck,
And others put their faith in their ability to pass the buck,
In short, the world is filled with people trying to achieve success,
And half of them think they'll get it by saying No and half of
    them by saying Yes,
And if all the ones who say No said Yes, and vice versa,
    such is the fate of humanity that ninety-nine per cent of
    them still wouldn't be any better off than they were before,
Which perhaps is just as well because if everybody was a success
    nobody could be contemptuous of anybody else and every-
    body would start in all over again trying to be a bigger
    success than everybody else so they would have somebody
    to be contemptuous of and so on forevermore,
Because when people start hitching their wagons to a star,
That's the way they are.

Ogden Nash

Confessions of a Born Spectator

One infant grows up and becomes a jockey,
Another plays basketball or hockey,
This one the prize ring hastes to enter,
That one becomes a tackle[1] or center.[1]
I'm just as glad as glad can be
That I'm not them, that they're not me.

With all my heart do I admire
Athletes who sweat for fun or hire,
Who take the field in gaudy pomp
And maim each other as they romp;
My limp and bashful spirit feeds
On other people's heroic deeds.

[1] Positions in American football.

Now A runs ninety yards to score;
B knocks the champion to the floor;
C, risking vertebrae and spine,
Lashes his steed across the line.
You'd think my ego it would please
To swap positions with one of these.

Well, ego might be pleased enough,
But zealous athletes play so rough;
They do not ever, in their dealings,
Consider one another's feelings.
I'm glad that when my struggle begins
Twixt prudence and ego, prudence wins.

When swollen eye meets gnarled fist,
When snaps the knee, and cracks the wrist,
When calm officialdom demands,
Is there a doctor in the stands?
My soul in true thanksgiving speaks
For this most modest of physiques.

Athletes, I'll drink to you or eat with you,
Or anything except compete with you;
Buy tickets worth their weight in radium
To watch you gambol in a stadium,
And reassure myself anew
That you're not me and I'm not you.

Ogden Nash

This is going to hurt just a little bit

One thing I like less than most things is sitting in a dentist chair
    with my mouth wide open,

And that I will never have to do it again is a hope that I am
    against hope hopen.

Because some tortures are physical and some are mental,

But the one that is both is dental.

It is hard to be self-possessed

With your jaw digging into your chest,

So hard to retain your calm

When your fingernails are making serious alterations in your life
    line or love line or some other important line in your palm;

So hard to give your usual effect of cheery benignity

When you know your position is one of the two or three in
    life most lacking in dignity.

And your mouth is like a section of road that is being worked on,

And it is all cluttered up with stone crushers and concrete mixers
    and drills and steam rollers and there isn't a nerve in your
    head that you aren't being irked on.

Oh, some people are unfortunate enough to be strung up by
    thumbs,

And others have things done to their gums,

And your teeth are supposed to be being polished,

But you have reason to believe they are being demolished,

And the circumstance that adds most to your terror

Is that it's all done with a mirror,

Because the dentist may be a bear, or as the Romans used to say,
    only they were referring to a feminine bear when they said
    it, an ursa,

But all the same how can you be sure when he takes his crowbar
    in one hand and mirror in the other he won't get mixed up,

the way you do when you try to tie a bow tie with the aid
of a mirror, and forget that left is right and vice versa?
And then at last he says That will be all; but it isn't because he
then coats your mouth from cellar to roof
With something that I suspect is generally used to put a shine on
a horse's hoof,
And you totter to your feet and think, Well it's all over now and
after all it was only this once,
And he says come back in three monce.
And this, O Fate, is I think the most vicious circle that thou ever
sentest,
That Man has to go continually to the dentist to keep his teeth
in good condition when the chief reason he wants his teeth in
good condition is so that he won't have to go to the dentist.

Ogden Nash

Portrait of a Machine

What nudity as beautiful as this
Obedient monster purring at its toil;
These naked iron muscles dripping oil,
And the sure-fingered rods that never miss?
This long and shining flank of metal is
Magic that greasy labour cannot spoil;
While this vast engine that could rend the soil
Conceals its fury with a gentle hiss.
It does not vent its loathing, it does not turn
Upon its makers with destroying hate.
It bears a deeper malice; lives to earn
Its master's bread and laughs to see this great
Lord of the earth, who rules but cannot learn,
Become the slave of what his slaves create.

Louis Untermeyer

On a Subway Express

I, who have lost the stars, the sod,
  For chilling pave and cheerless light,
Have made my meeting-place with God
  A new and nether Night —

Have found a fane where thunder fills
  Loud caverns, tremulous; — and these
Atone me for my reverend hills
  And moonlit silences.

A figment in the crowded dark,
  Where men sit muted by the roar,
I ride upon the whirring Spark
  Beneath the city's floor.

In this dim firmament, the stars
  Whir by in blazing files and tiers;
Kin meteors graze our flying bars,
  Amid the spinning spheres.

Speed! Speed! until the quivering rails
  Flash silver where the headlight gleams,
As when on lakes the moon impales
  The waves upon its beams.

Life throbs about me, yet I stand
  Outgazing on majestic Power;
Death rides with me, on either hand,
  In my communion hour.

You that 'neath country skies can pray,
   Scoff not at me — the city clod; —
My only respite of the Day
   Is this wild ride — with God.

Chester Firkins

Map of My Country

A map of my native country is all edges,
The shore touching sea, the easy impartial rivers
Splitting the local boundary lines, round hills in two townships,
Blue ponds interrupting the careful county shapes.
The Mississippi runs down the middle. Cape Cod. The Gulf.
Nebraska is on latitude forty. Kansas is west of Missouri.

When I was a child, I drew it, from memory,
A game in the schoolroom, naming the big cities right.

Cloud shadows were not shown, nor where winter whitens,
Nor the wide road the day's wind takes.

None of the tall letters told my grandfather's name.
Nothing said, Here they see in clear air a hundred miles.
Here they go to bed early. They fear snow here.
Oak trees and maple boughs I had seen on the long hillsides
Changing color, and laurel, and bayberry, were never mapped.
Geography told only capitals and state lines.

I have come a long way using other men's maps for the turnings.
I have a long way to go.
It is time I drew the map again,
Spread with the broad colors of life, and words of my own
Saying, Here the people worked hard, and died for the wrong
    reasons.

Here wild strawberries tell the time of year.
I could not sleep, here, while bell-buoys beyond the surf rang.
Here trains passed in the night, crying of distance,
Calling to cities far away, listening for an answer.

On my own map of my own country
I shall show where there were never wars,
And plot the changed way I hear men speak in the west,
Words in the south slower, and food different.
Not the court-houses seen floodlighted at night from trains,
But the local stone built into housewalls,
And barns telling the traveler where he is
By the slant of the roof, the color of the paint.
Not monuments. Not the battlefields famous in school.
But Thoreau's pond,[1] and Huckleberry Finn's island.
I shall name an unhistorical hill three boys climbed one morning.
Lines indicate my few journeys,
And the long way letters come from absent friends.

Forest is where green fern cooled me under the big trees.
Ocean is where I ran in the white drag of waves on white sand.
Music is what I heard in a country house while hearts broke,
Not knowing they were breaking, and Brahms wrote it.

All that I remember happened to me here.
This is the known world.
I shall make a star here for a man who died too young.
Here, and here, in gold, I shall mark two towns
Famous for nothing, except that I have been happy in them.

John Holmes

[1] Walden Pond, near Concord, where Thoreau built himself a hut and tried, for a time, to live 'a life of simplicity, independence, magnanimity, and trust'.

The Fish

I caught a tremendous fish
and held him beside the boat
half out of water, with my hook
fast in a corner of his mouth.
He didn't fight.
He hadn't fought at all.
He hung a grunting weight,
battered and venerable
and homely. Here and there
his brown skin hung in strips
like ancient wall-paper,
and its pattern of darker brown
was like wall-paper:
shapes like full-blown roses
stained and lost through age.
He was speckled with barnacles,
fine rosettes of lime,
and infested
with tiny white sea-lice,
and underneath two or three
rags of green weed hung down.
While his gills were breathing in
the terrible oxygen
— the frightening gills,
fresh and crisp with blood,
that can cut so badly —
I thought of the coarse white flesh
packed in like feathers,
the big bones and the little bones,
the dramatic reds and blacks

of his shiny entrails,
and the pink swim-bladder
like a big peony.
I looked into his eyes
which were far larger than mine
but shallower, and yellowed,
the irises backed and packed
with tarnished tinfoil
seen through lenses
of old scratched isinglass.
They shifted a little, but not
to return my stare.
– It was more like the tipping
of an object toward the light.
I admired his sullen face,
the mechanism of his jaw,
and then I saw
that from his lower lip
– if you could call it a lip –
grim, wet, and weapon-like,
hung five old pieces of fish-line,
or four and a wire leader
with the swivel still attached,
with all their five big hooks
grown firmly in his mouth.
A green line, frayed at the end
where he broke it, two heavier lines,
and a fine black thread
still crimped from the strain and snap
when it broke and he got away.
Like medals with their ribbons
frayed and wavering,

a five-haired beard of wisdom
trailing from his aching jaw.
I stared and stared
and victory filled up
the little rented boat,
from the pool of bilge
where oil had spread a rainbow
around the rusted engine
to the bailer rusted orange,
the sun-cracked thwarts,
the oarlocks on their strings,
the gunnels — until everything
was rainbow, rainbow, rainbow!
And I let the fish go.

Elizabeth Bishop

Portrait

The clear brown eyes, kindly and alert, with 12-20 vision, give
confident regard to the passing world through R. K. Lam-
pert & Company lenses framed in gold;
His soul, however, is all his own;
Arndt Brothers necktie and hat (with feather) supply a touch of
youth.

With his soul his own, he drives, drives, chats and drives,
The first and second bicuspids, lower right, replaced by bridge-
work, while two incisors have porcelain crowns;

(Render unto Federal, state and city Caesar, but not unto time;
Render nothing unto time until Amalgamated Death serves
final notice, in proper form;

The vault is read;

The will has been drawn by Clagget, Clagget, Clagget & Brown;

The policies are adequate, Confidential's best, reimbursing for disability, partial or complete, with double indemnity should the end be a pure and simple accident)

Nothing unto time,

Nothing unto change, nothing unto fate,

Nothing unto you, and nothing unto me, or to any other known or unknown party or parties, living or deceased;

But Mercury shoes, with special arch supporters, take much of the wear and tear;

On the course, a custombuilt driver corrects a tendency to slice;

Love's ravages have been repaired (it was a textbook case) by Drs Schultz, Lightner, Mannheim, and Goode,

While all of it is enclosed in excellent tweed, with Mr Baumer's personal attention to the shoulders and waist;

And all of it now roving, chatting amiably through space in a Plymouth 6,

With his soul (his own) at peace, soothed by Walter Lippmann,[1] and sustained by Haig & Haig.[2]

Kenneth Fearing

The Serf

Though born in South Africa, Roy Campbell lived much of his life in Spain and the South of France. Always adventurous, he fought in three wars: his 'peaceful' occupations included work as a cowboy, a fisherman and even a bullfighter.

[1] A famous American commentator.
[2] A firm of whisky distillers: here their product.

His naked skin clothed in the torrid mist
That puffs in smoke around the patient hooves,
The ploughman drives, a slow somnambulist,
And through the green his crimson furrow grooves
His heart, more deeply than he wounds the plain,
Long by the rasping share of insult torn,
Red clod, to which the war-cry once was rain
And tribal spears the fatal sheaves of corn,
Lies fallow now. But as the turf divides
I see in the slow progress of his strides
Over the toppled clods and falling flowers,
The timeless, surly patience of the serf
That moves the nearest to the naked earth
And ploughs down palaces, and thrones, and towers.

Roy Campbell

The Zebras

From the dark woods that breathe of fallen showers,
Harnessed with level rays in golden reins,
The zebras draw the dawn across the plains
Wading knee-deep among the scarlet flowers.
The sunlight, zithering their flanks with fire,
Flashes between the shadows as they pass
Barred with electric tremors through the grass
Like wind along the gold strings of a lyre.

Into the flushed air snorting rosy plumes
That smoulder round their feet in drifting fumes,
With dove-like voices call the distant fillies,
While round the herds the stallion wheels his flight,
Engine of beauty volted with delight,
To roll his mare among the trampled lilies.

Roy Campbell

Horses on the Camargue

The Camargue is an extensive and desolate plain in France around the Rhône delta. Herds of wild horses roam there and are only occasionally rounded up to be tamed and put to work. The unattractive nature of the region is made worse by the Mistral, a dry stormy wind which, in winter and spring, blows down the Rhône Valley for days on end, and sweeps across the Camargue.

In the grey wastes of dread,
The haunt of shattered gulls where nothing moves
But in a shroud of silence like the dead,
I heard a sudden harmony of hooves,
And, turning, saw afar
A hundred snowy horses unconfined,
The silver runaways of Neptune's car
Racing, spray-curled, like waves before the wind.
Sons of the Mistral, fleet
As him with whose strong gusts they love to flee,
Who shod the flying thunders on their feet
And plumed them with the snortings of the sea;
Theirs is no earthly breed
Who only haunt the verges of the earth
And only on the sea's salt herbage feed —
Surely the great white breakers gave them birth.
For when for years a slave,
A horse of the Camargue, in alien lands,
Should catch some far-off fragrance of the wave
Carried far inland from his native sands,
Many have told the tale
Of how in fury, foaming at the rein,
He hurls his rider; and with lifted tail,
With coal-red eyes and cataracting mane,

Heading his course for home,
Though sixty foreign leagues before him sweep,
Will never rest until he breathes the foam
And hears the native thunder of the deep.
But when the great gusts rise
And lash their anger on these arid coasts,
When the scared gulls career with mournful cries
And whirl across the waste like driven ghosts:
When hail and fire converge,
The only souls to which they strike no pain
Are the white-crested fillies of the surge
And the white horses of the windy plain.
Then in their strength and pride
The stallions of the wilderness rejoice;
They feel their Master's trident[1] in their side,
And high and shrill they answer to his voice.
With white tails smoking free,
Long streaming manes, and arching necks, they show
Their kinship to their sisters of the sea —
And forward hurl their thunderbolts of snow.
Still out of hardship bred,
Spirits of power and beauty and delight
Have ever on such frugal pastures fed
And loved to course with tempests through the night.

Roy Campbell

[1] Neptune traditionally carries a trident. The riders who round up the herds also use tridents to control the wild horses.

Rain in Africa

Lewis Sowden has lived much of his life in the South African gold-fields where he now works as a journalist.

> The beat of the rain
> on the street is the meeting
> of hammer and heat
> over concrete and stone;
> like the thrashing of fire
> in the crop, or the clatter
> on anvil top,
> or the crashing of trees
> at the woodcutter's beat
> again and again
>
> The beat of the rain
> on the street is repeated
> in afternoon feet
> that emerge and recede
> at the verge of the wet,
> on teetering toes
> and slithering shoes,
> and shuffle to shelter
> in doorway and lane.
>
> The beat of the rain
> on roadway and roofs
> like the scampering hoofs
> of the stampeding herds,
> of the bleating of flocks
> in dismay; like the tread

of brigades in retreat;
or the beat in the brain
of remorse and defeat;
or regretting too late;
or the tumult of hearts
when lovers must part,
is the beat of the rain
on the street.

The shuddering skies
that shutter their eyes
at the rudderless clouds,
the Mother of the Thunder
she tears them asunder
and laughs in the shrouds.
With glittering streak
she shatters their van,
and scatters their cargo
from Virgo to Ram,
with shriek upon shriek
at the sight of the plunder.

The spluttering rain
over grassland and plain
plucks open the roots
in the ruts and the sluits,
and the galloping waters
that jostle and rumble
through rustle of branches
shout over the spray,
and meet in the gutters
to mutter and bray,
where clutter the leaves

that littered the drains
with Autumn's remains.
The ditches are tumbling
with debris of day.

Then the light reaches out
from the doors of the night —
All heaven is blest.
All anger is spent
before the descent
of the day in the west.
The sky is the sea,
the world sailing free
on billow and crest,
with Faith to steer it.
The sky is the breast
where flutters the spirit
for succour and rest.
    The Earth is its nest.

Lewis Sowden

A Mayor

The Mayor he was a Councillor
Of weight (himself had said it).
The Mayor he was a self-made man
And loved to get the credit.

One day I met him on the Square
And hailed him like a freeman.
'Good morning!' merrily I said,
'Good morning, Mr Nieman.'

The Mayor he turned his heavy head
Sedately. 'Please remember,
From now on I remain,' he said,
'Mr Mayor till next November.'

So ever since when I salute
That Civic Dignita-a-ry,
I always take especial care
To greet him tempora-a-ry.

I never know his native name;
I faultlessly remember
To call him — Mr Mayor Until
The Following November.

Lewis Sowden

High-diving

The first time Speedy lighted on my thoughts
Was in a letter to the Editor,
On a crumpled piece of paper quarto
Left on my desk. The typesetter,
As interested as I, kept talking,
Remembering, till Speedy's story
Started my own reflections, waking
Ideas from a neglected quarry
Of the days, till I recognized
The case of Speedy as familiarized
By many instances, a case
Of death by accident quite commonplace
(The way the Coroner set the matter out),
But not without significance,
The kind that often attends on chance —
Or seeming chance; for there's the doubt.

Speedy — that was only his stage-name,
Painted on bills in letters of flame,
Part of the act. No one recalls
Any other. If a man takes a name in the halls
It sticks, if at all. That's fame.
Speedy was a high-diver.
Every evening about eight, or maybe nine,
He'd climb a hundred wavering feet
To top a mast above the skyline.
You could see that part of the show from the street
For nothing, see him in the lime-light,
Stretching, bending, disdaining the earth,
Giving the patrons their money's worth
And the dead-heads an appetite.

Then, poising himself in mid-air,
At the last rat-a-plan of the gong
And a thousand faces in upward gaze,
He'd leap from his perch headlong
And dive into a pool six feet square,
Surrounded by a paraffin blaze
To make it look more hazardous.
You could hear the splash from the street and the crash of the
        gong again,
And a thousand voices shouting praise
To see a man so nearly kill himself.
And if each night he made a fiver,
That was good money for a high-diver
In those days.

But Speedy, like many a wiser man,
Was ambitious. Higher and higher

He raised his mast-head, took a flier
From hundred and twenty feet — or higher —
Miscalculated — a gust, a whim,
A second out would have done for him —
And landed beside the water-pit.
No splash that night, no rat-a-plan,
And no tears at the end of it.

Next day the papers told the news
Under headlines suitably large, even the views
Of the journalist from his ringside chair
Moved by proximity to give
His feelings in print. High-diving, he implied,
That was how Speedy had chosen to live.
He erred, of course, as journalists often do,
Concerned as they are with appearances,
And missing the paradox inherent
In all things by a whole galley or two.
The point was not that Speedy had chosen how to live,
But how to die. The alternative
It was that drew him, inquisitive
Of the last adventure, and how to find it,
Knowing that where Life was most alive
There Death stood close behind it
Ready to grasp the hand that missed.

So Speedy contemplating his dive;
So on his tight-wire the equilibrist;
So the mountain climber on his ledge;
So the explorer on Polar wedge;
So the airman at Earth's outer edge.

So every man who seeks the living breath
Too passionately, and is amazed in death.

Lewis Sowden

Nightpiece

Three men came talking up the road
And still 'to-morrow' was the word.

The night was clear with the lamps' glitter.
The first man spoke and his voice was bitter.

'To-morrow like another day
I draw the dole and rust away.'

The second one said scared and low,
'To-morrow I may have to go.'

And the two spoke never another word
But drew together and looked at the third,

And the third man said, 'If to-morrow exists,
It's a day of streets like rivers of fists,

It's the end of crawling, the end of the doles,
And men are treated as human souls.'

I stood in the doorway and heard these things
As the three came past with the step of kings.

John Manifold

Men in Green

The Australian and New Zealand troops fighting the Japanese (and the climate) in Burma and New Guinea were often supplied, reinforced and relieved by air, owing to the impassable nature of the jungle. Dobadura was an airfield in New Guinea from which such operations were carried out.

Oh, there were fifteen men in green,
Each with a tommy-gun,
Who leapt into my plane at dawn;
We rose to meet the sun.

We set our course towards the east
And climbed with the day
Till the ribbed jungle underneath
Like a giant fossil lay.

We climbed towards the distant range,
Where two white paws of cloud
Clutched at the shoulders of the pass;
The green men laughed aloud.

They did not fear the ape-like cloud
That climbed the mountain crest
And hung from ropes invisible
With lightning in its breast.

They did not fear the summer's sun
In whose hot centre lie
A hundred hissing cannon shells
For the unwatchful eye.

143

And when on Dobadura's field
We landed, each man raised
His thumb towards the open sky;
But to their right I gazed.

For fifteen men in jungle green
Rose from the kunai grass
And came towards the plane. My men
In silence watched them pass;
It seemed they looked upon themselves
In Time's prophetic glass.

Oh, there were some leaned on a stick
And some on stretchers lay,
But few walked on their own two feet
In the early green of day.

(They did not heed the ape-like cloud
That climbed the mountain crest;
They did not fear the summer's sun
With bullets for their breast.)

Their eyes were bright, their looks were dull;
Their skin had turned to clay.
Nature had met them in the night
And stalked them in the day.

And I think still of men in green
On the Sponta track,
With fifteen spitting tommy-guns
To keep the jungle back.

David Campbell

Life-saver

The east coast of Australia has famous stretches of beach, such as Bondi Beach near Sydney, though the surf and occasionally the sharks can make the bathing dangerous. The life-guard or life-saver, distinguished by his swimming prowess and magnificent physique, is a familiar figure on such beaches.

He was brought up out of the sea,
His tall body dead.
He was carried shoulder high
Between the sea and the sky.
The sun and the water trembled down
From his fingers and from the brown
Valley between his shoulders; and the spray
Fell before him as he passed on his way.

His eyes were dead, and his lips
Closed on death, and his feet
Chained with death, and his hands
Cold with death. He is one now with ships
And the bones of pirate bands
Steeped in salt and knavery.
One with fish and weed and pearl
And the long lonely beat
Of the waves that curl
On shell and rock and sand
Of a deep drowned land.

He was carried shoulder high
Up the alleys of the sun;
And the heat
Washed him over from his head to his feet,

But you cannot give the body back breath
With a flagon full of sun.
He is drowned, the tall one.
Thin brother Death
Has him by the throat
On the sand, in the sun.

Elizabeth Riddell

Request to a Year

If the year is meditating a suitable gift,
I should like it to be the attitude
of my great-great-grandmother,
legendary devotee of the arts,

who, having had eight children
and little opportunity for painting pictures,
sat one day on a high rock
beside a river in Switzerland

and from a difficult distance viewed
her second son, balanced on a small ice-floe,
drift down the current towards a waterfall
that struck rock-bottom eighty feet below,

while her second daughter, impeded,
no doubt, by the petticoats of the day,
stretched out a last-hope alpenstock
(which luckily later caught him on his way).

Nothing, it was evident, could be done;
and with the artist's isolating eye
my great-great-grandmother hastily sketched the scene.
The sketch survives to prove the story by.

Year, if you have no Mother's Day present planned,
reach back and bring me the firmness of her hand.

Judith Wright

Res Publica[1]

They bled a bullock, and stripped the hide,
Cast to the dogs what they could not use;
Tanned the skin that the sun had dried,
And made the leather for Caesar's shoes.

A shivering lamb was shorn in Spain;
The wool was teased and combed and dressed.
They washed it clean of the pasture stain,
And wove a toga for Caesar's breast.

A pig that rooted acorns saw
The shrub resent as they plucked the bough,
And watched the shadows of men withdraw
Bearing the laurel for Caesar's brow.

They dug the metal to fill the mould,
And fed the flame in a place apart,
Ground the edge when the steel was cold,
And made the dagger for Caesar's heart.

J. A. R. McKellar

[1] Literally, the State: here the individuals who go to make it.

Death of a Whale

When the mouse died, there was a sort of pity;
The tiny, delicate creature made for grief.
Yesterday, instead, the dead whale on the reef
Drew an excited multitude to the jetty.
How must a whale die to wring a tear?
Lugubrious death of a whale; the big
Feast for the gulls and sharks; the tug
Of the tide simulating life still there,
Until the air, polluted, swings this way
Like a door ajar from a slaughterhouse.
Pooh! pooh! spare us, give us the death of a mouse
By its tiny hole; not this in our lovely bay.
— Sorry, we are, too, when a child dies:
But at the immolation of a race, who cries?

John Blight

In the Day's Work

We left the homestead at break of day,
    And into the desert we rode away.
There was arid rock on either hand,
Veiled with drifting, red-brown sand,
And nothing the aching silence stirred,
No insect's chirr nor song of bird,
Just desolate, silent loneliness;
The creak of leather, the ashy hiss
Of loose sand falling to Gunnar's tread
Were all that moved, in that land of dread.
All river-beds were parched and dry,
Their hot rocks bare to the blazing sky;

And I'd dream at night of water-falls,
Dashing down their rocky walls;
Of rivers flowing, deep and cool,
And many a placid, woodland pool,
Where lilies bloomed at the water's brink,
And shy bush-creatures stooped to drink.
Then I'd wake, to heat, and sand, and thirst
In that desolate land that God had cursed.
On the desert's rim one pool we found,
Choked with beasts that had long lain drowned.
My nigger dropped from his horse with a shout,
Raked rotting hides and bones all out,
Gulping the fetid ooze of the soak,
While I sat and cursed, in a strangled croak.
My throat was parched, as dry as hell,
But I dared not drink from that reeking well.
So we turned our faces south again,
Where heat waves danced on the arid plain,
On the hard brown earth, 'neath a brazen sky,
Where wings of Death went drifting by.

Jesse Sinclair Litchfield

Darlingford

Blazing tropical sunshine
On a hard, white dusty road
That curves round and round
Following the craggy coastline;
Coconut trees fringing the coast,
Thousands and thousands
Of beautiful coconut trees,

Their green and brown arms
Reaching out in all directions —
Reaching up to high heaven
And sparkling in the sunshine.
Sea coast, rocky sea coast,
Rocky palm-fringed coastline;
Brown-black rocks,
White sea-foam spraying the rocks;
Waves, sparkling waves
Dancing merrily with the breeze;
The incessant song
Of the mighty sea,
A white sail — far out
Far, far out at sea;
A tiny sailing boat —
White sails all glittering
Flirting with the bright rays
Of the soon setting sun,
Trying to escape their kisses,
In vain — and the jealous winds
Waft her on, on, out to sea
Till sunset; then weary
Of their battle with the sun
The tired winds
Fold themselves to sleep
And the noble craft
No longer idolized
By her two violent lovers
Drifts slowly into port
In the pale moonlight;
Gone are the violent caresses
Of the sun and restless winds —

She nestles in the cool embrace
Of quiet waves
And tender moonlight
Southern silvery moonlight
Shining from a pale heaven
Upon a hard, white, dusty road
That curves round and round
Following the craggy coastline
Of Jamaica's southern shore.

Una Marson

Nature

We have neither Summer nor Winter
Neither Autumn nor Spring.

We have instead the days
When gold sun shines on the lush green canefields —
Magnificently.

The days when the rain beats like bullets on the roofs
And there is no sound but the swish of water in the gullies
And trees struggling in the high Jamaica winds.

Also there are the days when the leaves fade from off guango
    trees
And the reaped canefields lie bare and fallow in the sun.

But best of all there are the days when the mango and the
    logwood blossoms.

When the bushes are full of the sound of bees and the scent of
    honey,

When the tall grass sways and shivers to the slightest breath of air,

When the buttercups have paved the earth with yellow stars
And beauty comes suddenly and the rains have gone.

H. D. Carberry

Prayer of a Black Boy

The insistent demand for education made by West Indians and Africans of all races and creeds is one of the phenomena of our time. Nonetheless all of us, black and white, feel from time to time as this black boy does.

Lord, I am so tired.
Tired I entered this world.
Far have I wandered since the cock crew,
And the road to school is steep.
Lord, I do not want to go into their school,
Please help me that I need not go again.
I want to follow father into the cool gorges.
When the night is hovering over magic forests
Where spirits play before the dawn.
Barefoot, I want to tread the red-hot paths,
That boil in midday sun,
And then lie down to sleep beneath a Mango tree.
And I want to wake up only
When down there the white man's siren starts to howl,
And the factory,
A ship on the sugarfields,
Lands and spits its crew,
Of black workers into the landscape ...
Lord, I do not want to go into their school,

Please help me that I need not go again,
It's true, they say a little negro ought to go,
So that he might become
Just like the gentlemen of the city,
So that he might become a real gentleman.
But I, I do not want to become
A gentleman of the city, or as they call it
A real gentleman.
I'd rather stroll along the sugar stores
Where the tight sacks are piled
With brown sugar, brown like my skin.
I'd rather listen — when the moon is whispering
Tenderly into the ear of cocopalms,
To what the old man who always smokes,
Recites with breaking voice during the night,
The stories of Samba and Master Hare
And many others more that are not found in any book.
Lord, the negroes have had too much work already,
Why should we learn again from foreign books,
About all kinds of things we've never seen?
And then, their school is far too sad,
Just as sad as these gentlemen of the city,
These real gentlemen
Who do not even know how to dance by the light of the moon,
Who do not even know how to walk on the flesh of their feet,
Who do not even know how to tell the tales of their fathers
By the light of their nightly fires.
O Lord, I do not want to go into their school again.

Guy Tirolien

The Heart to Carry On

Bertram Warr, born and educated in Canada, came to England and joined the R.A.F. in 1941. He was killed in action two years later while on a bombing raid.

Every morning from this home
I go to the aerodrome.
And at evening I return
Save when work is to be done.
Then we share the separate night
Half a continent apart.

Many endure worse than we:
Division means by years and seas.
Home and lover are contained,
Even cursed within their breast.

Leaving you now, with this kiss
May your sleep to-night be blest,
Shielded from the heart's alarms
Until morning I return.
Pray to-morrow I may be
Close, my love, within these arms,
And not lie dead in Germany.

Bertram Warr

Afterword

I have turned my reveries to rhyme
And dug my buried self
Out of the layers of the years,
Finding that what I'd cast aside

Was what I sought, and what I thought
Poor currency in the world
Was all that satisfied.

Oh I have written much
And much have torn,
And if I found a little praise,
A little scorn,
What I have wanted most
Was pleasure in the thing itself,
My own conviction of its worth,
And if that was little or counterfeit,
No praise could compensate.

Pleasure in the idea the moment of its birth
And the word that leaps to meet it;
Pleasure in the line that shapes a thought from feeling
Before I have well conceived it;
Pleasure in the phrase like evening star
Shining through the mist that hides it;
In the word that rings in a far belfry
And the wind misguides it.

So I have turned my reveries to rhyme
(Or half-rhyme)
And made a book of them,
And if they make a little sound
Or none,
All's one.
The joy was in the doing,
Not in having done.

Lewis Sowden

ACKNOWLEDGMENTS

Acknowledgments for permission to reprint copyright poems are due to the following authors, executors and publishers: —

The author and Hutchinson & Co. (Publishers) Ltd. for EMPERORS OF THE ISLAND from *Tenants of the House* by Dannie Abse; the author and Faber & Faber Ltd. for THE UNKNOWN CITIZEN from *Collected Shorter Poems* and CHORUS from *The Dog Beneath the Skin* by W. H. Auden, and the author and Curtis Brown Ltd. for DIALOGUE from *The Ascent of F.6*, also by W. H. Auden; the author and Faber & Faber Ltd. for ON A FRIEND'S ESCAPE from *Collected Poems* by George Barker; the author and Andrew Dakers Ltd. for THE HORNS OF LUD I from *The Galloping Centaur* by Frances Berry; the author and Houghton Miflin Company for THE FISH from *North & South* by E. Bishop; John Thompson for his poem DEATH OF A WHALE, first published in *The Bulletin*, Sydney, from *The Penguin Book of Australian Verse*; the author and William Collins, Sons & Co. Ltd. for THE PIKE from *Poems of Many Years* by Edmund Blunden; the author and J. M. Dent & Sons Ltd. for BEAUTY NEVER VISITS MINING PLACES, NAY, THERE'S NEITHER HOPE NOR EASE and AS I CAME HOME FROM LABOUR from *Out of the Coalfields* by F. C. Boden; the author and Chatto & Windus Ltd. for MEN IN GREEN from *Speak With The Sun* by David Campbell; Mrs Roy Campbell for THE SERF and THE ZEBRAS from *Collected Poems*, and HORSES ON THE CAMARGUE from *Adamastor* by Roy Campbell; The Poetry League of Jamaica for EPITAPH and NATURE by H. D. Carberry from *The Treasury of Jamaican Verse*; the author and J. M. Dent & Sons Ltd. for THE SON from *Straight or Curly* and THE SWANS from *Collected Poems* by Clifford Dyment; the author and Faber & Faber Ltd. for THE DRY SALVAGES IV and CHORUS from *The Rock* by T. S. Eliot; D. J. Enright and Secker & Warburg Ltd. for THE MONUMENTS OF HIROSHIMA from *Bread Rather Than Blossoms*; Kenneth Fearing and the Indiana University Press for PORTRAIT from *Collected Poems*; Robert Frost, Jonathan Cape Ltd. and Messrs. Henry Holt & Co. Inc. for THE DEATH OF THE HIRED MAN, TWO TRAMPS IN MUD TIME, OUT — OUT, A CONSIDERABLE SPECK and THE EXPOSED NEST from *The Complete Poems of Robert Frost*; Robert Graves and Cassell & Co. Ltd. for 1805, THE GENERAL ELLIOTT, LOLLOCKS, WARNING TO CHILDREN, WELLCOME TO THE CAVES OF ARTA, TRAVELLER'S CURSE AFTER MISDIRECTION and FLYING CROOKED from

Collected Poems, 1959; J. C. Hall for WAR from *The Summer Dance* published by John Lehmann Ltd.; The Marvell Press for AT GRASS, WIRES, BORN YESTERDAY and TOADS from *The Less Deceived* by Philip Larkin; John Holmes and Duell, Sloan & Pearce Inc. for MAP OF MY COUNTRY I from *Map of my Country*, Copyright 1943 by John Holmes; the executors of John Jarmain and William Collins Sons & Co. Ltd. for PRISONERS OF WAR and EL ALAMEIN from *Poems*; James Kirkup and the Oxford University Press for WREATH MAKERS: LEEDS MARKET from *A Correct Compassion*; the Estate of the late Frieda Lawrence and Messrs. William Heinemann Ltd. for THE MOUNTAIN LION from *Collected Poems* by D. H. Lawrence; Alun Lewis and George Allen & Unwin Ltd. for ALL DAY IT HAS RAINED and THE MOUNTAINS OVER ABERDARE from *Raider's Dawn* and SACCO WRITES TO HIS SON from *Ha! Ha! Among the Trumpets*; C. Day Lewis and Jonathan Cape Ltd. for THE MAGNETIC MOUNTAIN I, 2, THE MAGNETIC MOUNTAIN II, 9, and THE MAGNETIC MOUNTAIN III, 25 from *Collected Poems* and THE MISFIT, TWO TRAVELLERS and A HARD FROST from *Poems 1943-1947*.

Louis Macneice and Faber & Faber Ltd. for TO THE PUBLIC and JIGSAW II from *Visitations*, PRAYER BEFORE BIRTH, CHRISTMAS SHOPPING, THE BRITISH MUSEUM READING ROOM, PASSAGE STEAMER, TURF-STACKS, THE CYCLIST and SWING-SONG from *Collected Poems* and two extracts from *Autumn Journal*; J. A. R. McKellar and Angus & Robertson Ltd. for RES PUBLICA; John Manifold, The John Day Co. Inc. and Dennis Dobson Ltd. for NIGHTPIECE from *Selected Verse*; Una Marson and The Poetry League of Jamaica for DARLINGFORD from *The Treasury of Jamaican Verse*; Edwin Muir and Faber & Faber Ltd. for THE CASTLE, THE KILLING and SUBURBAN DREAM from *Collected Poems*; Ogden Nash for ENGLAND EXPECTS, CONFESSIONS OF A BORN SPECTATOR and THIS IS GOING TO HURT JUST A LITTLE BIT from *I'm a Stranger Here Myself* and KINDLY UNHITCH THAT STAR, BUDDY from *Many Long Years Ago*; John Pudney and Putnam & Co. Ltd. for FOR JOHNNY, SECURITY, MISSING, LOVE OF COUNTRY I, LOVE OF COUNTRY II and AUNTS WATCHING TELEVISION from *Collected Poems*; Herbert Read and Faber & Faber Ltd. for TO A CONSCRIPT OF 1940, THE IVY AND THE ASH and NIGHT RIDE from *Collected Poems*; Elizabeth Riddell and Angus & Robertson Ltd. for LIFE-SAVER from *Australian Poetry 1942*; Michael Roberts and Faber & Faber Ltd. for H.M.S. HERO, LA MEIJE 1937, THE IMAGES OF DEATH and 'ALREADY' SAID MY HOST from *Collected Poems*; W. R. Rodgers and Martin Secker & Warburg Ltd. for STORMY DAY from *Awake! And Other Poems*; Alan

Ross and Hamish Hamilton Ltd. for STANLEY MATTHEWS and SLOW TRAIN TO PORTSMOUTH from *To Whom It May Concern*; Carl Sandburg and Henry Holt & Co. Inc. for CHICAGO from *Chicago Poems*, Copyright 1916 by Henry Holt & Co. Inc., Copyright 1944 by Carl Sandburg; Carl Sandburg and Harcourt, Brace & Co. Inc. for FOUR PRELUDES ON PLAY- THINGS OF THE WIND from *Smoke and Steel*, Copyright 1920 by Harcourt, Brace & Co. Inc., renewed by Carl Sandburg; Siegfried Sassoon for AT THE CENOTAPH, THOUGHTS IN 1932 and THE CASE FOR THE MINERS from *Collected Poems*; Lewis Sowden and Robert Hale Ltd. for RAIN IN AFRICA, A MAYOR, HIGH DIVING and AFTERWORD from *Poems With A Flute*; Stephen Spender and Faber & Faber Ltd. for THE EXPRESS, PYLONS, PORT BOU and ULTIMA RATIO REGUM from *Collected Poems*; Margaret Stanley- Wrench and Outposts Publications for AN OLD MAN'S HANDS from *Out- posts*; the executors of the late Dylan Thomas and J. M. Dent & Sons Ltd. for AND DEATH SHALL HAVE NO DOMINION, THE HAND THAT SIGNED THE PAPER, POEM IN OCTOBER and THE HUNCHBACK IN THE PARK from *Collected Poems* by Dylan Thomas; the author and M. Leopold Sédar Senghor for PRAYER OF A BLACK BOY by Guy Tirolien; Raymond Tong for AFRICAN BEGGAR from *New Poems, 1954*; R. C. Trevelyan and Chatto & Windus Ltd. for THE AIRMAN from *Aftermath*; Louis Untermeyer and Harcourt, Brace & Co. Inc. for PORTRAIT OF A MACHINE from *Roast Leviathan*, Copyright 1932 by Harcourt, Brace & Co. Inc., renewed by Louis Untermeyer; Mrs. B. H. Warr for THE HEART TO CARRY ON by Bertram Warr, published in *The Penguin Book of Canadian Verse*; John Wain for THIS ABOVE ALL IS PRECIOUS AND REMARKABLE, printed in *The Guinness Book of Poetry, 1958*; and Judith Wright and Angus & Roberts son Ltd. for REQUEST TO A YEAR from *The Two Fires*.

Every step has been taken to make the list of acknowledgments come prehensive, but in one case all efforts to trace the owner of the copyright failed. It is hoped that this omission from the list will be pardoned.

INDEX OF FIRST LINES